the ichi tree monkey
new and selected stories

BAMA

TRANSLATED BY N. RAVI SHANKER

SPEAKING
TIGER

SPEAKING TIGER BOOKS LLP
4381/4, Ansari Road, Daryaganj
New Delhi 110002

Published by Speaking Tiger Books in paperback 2021

Copyright © Bama Susairaj
Translation copyright © N. Ravi Shanker

ISBN: 978-93-89231-50-2
eISBN: 978-93-89231-49-6

10 9 8 7 6 5 4 3 2 1

This is a work of fiction. Names, characters, places and incidents either are the product of the author's imagination or are used fictitiously, and any resemblance to actual persons, living or dead, events or locales is entirely coincidental.

All rights reserved.
No part of this publication may be reproduced, transmitted, or stored in a retrieval system, in any form or by any means, electronic, mechanical, photocopying, recording or otherwise, without the prior permission of the publisher.

This book is sold subject to the condition that it shall not, by way of trade or otherwise, be lent, resold, hired out, or otherwise circulated, without the publisher's prior consent, in any form of binding or cover other than that in which it is published.

Bama teaches in a primary school in Uthiramerur near Chennai, Tamil Nadu. Her pathbreaking childhood memoir *Karukku* (1992) extablished her as a distinct voice in Dalit literature. The English translation of *Karukku* won the Crossword Prize in 2001. Bama is also the author of the widely acclaimed novels *Sangati* (1994) and *Vanmam* (2002) and the short story collections *Kisumbukkaran* (1996) and *Oru Tattavum Erumaiyum* (2003).

Ravi Shanker lives and works in Palakkad, Kerala. He regularly translates from Malayalam and Tamil into English. Also a poet, he has published three collections of poetry: *Architecture of Flesh*, *The Bullet Train and Other Loaded Poems* and *Kintsugi by Hadni*.

Contents

Pongal	7
Annachi	13
Harum-scarum Saar	21
Chilli Powder	35
Rich Girl	48
Those Days	57
Ponnuthayi	66
Half-sari	76
Freedom	86
Old Man and a Buffalo	95
The Ichi Tree Monkey	110
Stereotype	118
Single	125
The Ancharamanippoo Tree	132
Empty Nest	143

Pongal

Pongal after Pongal, Madasami would pay his respects to his landlord and do whatever he had to, as tradition demanded. It was thus that this Pongal, too, he collected whatever was required and got ready to go.

When he caught hold of the rooster, tied its legs together and hung it upside down, the stupid bird not only launched into a high-pitched crowing, fluttering its wings agitatedly, but also started shitting profusely.

'The idiot has chosen the right time to shit, just when I'm leaving for Ayya's house!' He cursed as he hoisted a large pumpkin onto his shoulder and held it firmly with one hand.

'Elai, Elavarasu, you pick up those two sugarcanes, your brother will carry the big bunch of bananas, your mother can bring the rice.'

Madasami would have been around fifty, with a figure that demanded attention. His limbs were so long they resembled bamboo sticks. Though greying, he had a thick mop of hair that grew in tight curls.

He had tried his hand at innumerable jobs in order to bring up the seven or eight children he had fathered.

People in the street used to say that there was no job he had not done.

He opened a teashop at the far end of the street, but had to close it down as it didn't work out well. He then tried selling beans and other eatables, hawking them in street after street. That, too, didn't work. Then he tried taking mango and jackfruit groves on lease during plantation season and failed in that, too. Now, for the last four or five years, he had been a farmhand on the leased-out lands of Ramasami Ayya.

One day I asked him, 'How is it, Mama, that you fail at every business you take up?'

He was livid. 'Now you're asking! These people gobble up whatever the other caste fellows sell but when I try selling the same, people say this is a Parayan teashop, this paniyaram is made by a Parayan, and they won't buy anything. That's why I had to stop,' he said bitterly.

They say that for some time he even tried brewing and selling illicit liquor. And for many days he was in such a bad state that there was not even kanji—rice gruel—to drink. When the other villagers bought meat, he would buy only the innards because they were cheap.

He didn't send his children to school, except for his middle son Esakkimuthu. 'Can one study well when one's belly is empty?' He sent them out to roll beedis instead. Don't know by what quirk of fate he spared his middle son, Esakkimuthu, from going to work and sent him to school. That fellow huffed and puffed his way past the tenth and also studied to be a teacher. But no job came his way. For the last two years, he had done whatever work he got on daily wages, wandering around looking for a steady job.

As Madasami started walking with the things he had collected, his wife Rakkamma and son Elavarasu followed him. Esakkimuthu alone stood his ground, not bothering to lift the bunch of bananas.

'Hey, you, pick it up and come along,' Madasami said impatiently, 'it's getting late.'

'Why do we have to take all this to the landlord? If we made a curry with them, we would have a hearty meal for once, at least,' replied Esakki.

Rakkamma intervened, 'Don't say that, son! We cannot change our customs. How will the landlord feel? They are people who have tasted good things, so they alone should eat them. When have we ever tasted them? We should stick to the old ways...seri, seri, let's start.' Saying this she rolled a seelai and placed it under the bundle on her head for support.

Madasami too paused and said, looking back, 'You don't understand a thing, even after studying! Talking like a child! Are we taking these to the landlord for nothing? He will give us something in return. Seri, now pick them up.'

Esakkimuthu didn't move. 'I want to hear what great thing he is going to do for us in return.'

'This fellow is really pig-headed! All these years we have been bringing back pongal rice from the landlord's house—haven't you eaten it? Why didn't you ask these questions then? That towel around your neck—the landlord only gave that. Can we go and ask him for accounts? What an ignorant boy you are!' exclaimed Madasami.

'For a small measure of pongal and a towel worth just ten rupees, are we so wretched that we have to give them a bird worth seventy-eighty rupees, a huge pumpkin, sugarcane worth ten rupees, a whole bunch of bananas and four measures of rice? Ei, if we ourselves cooked and consumed all this, wouldn't it be enough for us for four or five days?' Esakki persisted.

Immediately, Rakkamma said, 'Don't argue like this. Are we giving it to the landlord because he is starving?' As if he won't survive if we don't give him all this! We're just doing whatever is possible for us. And we only do it once a year. The wealth he has is enough for four generations. Now hurry up, idiot!'

'If we are paying him a visit during Pongal, isn't it right that he should also pay us a visit with his family during Deepavali or New Year? Does he ever do that?' Esakki asked again.

'This fellow seems bent upon arguing! Listen, look at the landlord's status, his prestige, his caste! How dare you say that he too should come to the Parayar street and see us! I was wrong to send you to school. We will be done for if your words reach the landlord's ears, he'll make our lives miserable. Now, are you coming or not?' Madasami glared at Esakkimuthu.

'I am not. You people shamelessly throw your dignity to the wind and go and fall at his feet. Here's your landlord's stupid towel.' Esakki threw the towel down, spat furiously and left.

'The way he behaves, it doesn't look like he'll go far. The fellow doesn't know how to survive.' Saying this, Madasami himself lifted the bananas and started walking, followed by Rakkamma and Elavarasu.

On the way, the things his son had said occupied Madasami's thoughts. As soon as they came to the landlord's house, while still on the street outside, tying his towel around his waist in supplication, Madasami announced, 'Ayya, we bow before you.'

The landlord, who had observed all this from the terrace, called out to his wife below, 'Vasantha, you accept what they have brought and send them away.' Having commanded her thus, he turned and went into his room.

Vasantha went out and said, 'Madasami, leave whatever you have brought on the doorstep and come to the back door. Cut a banana leaf and bring it along when you come.'

Madasami did as he was told. Leaving everything on the doorstep, he went to the backyard near the cowshed. There, he accepted the pongal that was served on the leaf he had taken along and, bundling it up, returned to the front door. Rakkamma transferred all the rice she had brought to the sack that the landlady had spread out and made a packet of the pongal her husband brought.

'Ayya, we are leaving,' Madasami said humbly, and Ayya from inside commanded him to leave instantly.

On the way home, Madasami recollected with much sadness, 'Etha, Rakkamma, the landlord didn't even give us a towel this time as he used to earlier.'

'I thought that too. Looks like there's something in what that fellow Esakki says,' Rakkamma replied.

When a bit of the pongal was served to Elavarasu, he ate it up quickly and licked his fingers afterwards. Madasami thought to himself, 'This boy licks his fingers like a child, but that Esakkimuthu refuses even to touch it!'

Reaching home, Madasami chewed on what Esakki had said like a cow chewing cud. 'What he said is right. Why did I go and call him stupid? Am I not a fool to have gone there and come back like this?' The more he thought about it, the angrier Madasami got with himself.

Esakkimuthu, who had reached home just then, thought his father was still annoyed with him, so he went and sat on the stone pounder that lay in the front yard.

Seeing him, a multitude of emotions rose up within Madasami. After a while he said, 'Listen, Rakku, dump that pongal in the cows' feeding tub and boil some ragi. I will go and buy some dried fish. Boiled ragi with dried fish curry will taste good!' Saying this he left quickly.

Hearing this, Esakkimuthu felt as happy as if he had actually had some pongal rice. Rakkamma couldn't understand what was going on, but she went to light the fire in the hearth. Esakkimuthu dumped the pongal in the feeding trough, but the buffaloes and other cattle, finding something strange in it, ignored the new stuff and drank only the water.

Annachi

'This fellow seems to be a mischievous one. Though his father and mother were such innocents, look how this donkey born to them has grown to be such a nuisance,' Even as Madathi said this with a great deal of anger, Muthurathnam went further, 'The boys from that family are all like this. The others at least you can adjust to, but this Ammasi, no adjustment is possible in his case. Such a headstrong fellow!'

'Who are you talking about, that grandson of that Irulayi? Yemma...was he not born from the ribs?' Thayamma, who was sitting nearby and cleaning the green gram, asked.

Ammasi was all of twenty. He was an odd one, just as street gossip had it. The elders did not like him at all, but the youngsters worshipped him.

He was good-looking, with a body that matched his age, and sported a dark moustache. Good physique. When he smiled, his teeth glittered like a kenda fish thrashing in the sun. What did he brush his teeth with! Though he kept arguing all the time, there was some logic to his arguments. Seeing him wandering around aimlessly one would think he was a good-for-nothing, but he was a knowledgeable boy.

There were complaints about him every day. I thought people were criticizing him like this only because they didn't know him well. Even with this latest incident, I felt what he had done was right. So I met him and asked him all about what had happened.

I saw him early in the morning on the way to the kamma-bank to take a shit. It was then that we spoke to each other. When I asked him what the matter was, he gave me a big smile and, smiling, related the incident.

'Ei, machan, tell me what's wrong with this? Yesterday I did the ridge-levelling work at that Parasuramu's fields and came home early in the morning. I drank some koozh as soon as I reached, and while I was drinking I decided I would go to Nettiyakallu and come back, so I boarded a bus...'

'You had some work in Nettiyakallu?' I asked him.

'Just listen, machan. That shopkeeper's kid told me there was some well-digging work there and I thought I'd try and get that job. When I tried to board the bus at our village bus stand, it was difficult, as there was a big crowd.'

'Did you pick a fight with someone while boarding the bus?'

'Now don't be a spoilsport, machan! You just carry on yourself without hearing what I'm saying! Now, listen without interrupting.'

Since I knew him well, I said, 'Seri, you proceed. I won't butt in.' I settled down to listen to what he had to say.

'Somehow I managed to squeeze my way through the crowd and found a seat on the bus. That Chandrasekhar also got onto the same bus. Now, ask me who this Chandrasekhar is? The same upper-caste landlord for whom my father does farm labour! What did he say as soon as he set eyes on me? Now, listen carefully. I will repeat the dialogue that took place between us:

"Elai...Are you not the son of that Madasami?"

"Sure, I am the son of Madasami."

"Elai...Haven't you recognized me?"

"I have, I know you very well. Are you not Chandrasekhar?"

Saying this, Ammasi lifted his lungi and taking a beedi out of the pocket of his under-shorts, lit it.

'You know why I lit this beedi?' he asked me. 'Didn't I speak to that Chandrasekhar just like this after lighting a beedi and blowing out smoke? I wanted to create the same effect now.'

'Seri, now carry on. Agreed, you are a good actor, but you're testing my patience,' I said a bit irritably.

'Okay, okay. So listen:

"Still sitting, even after recognizing me? Get up, let me sit."

"It was with great difficulty that I had squeezed through the crowd and managed to grab this seat and sit down," I said. *"I'm getting down at Nettiyakallu. I'll keep sitting till then. You can sit after that."*

"Elai...Nettiyakallu is right here, okay? Now get up, da, and stand aside. Is it right for you to keep sitting while your ayya is standing, not paying him due respect?"

"Did you say ayya? My ayya is ploughing your field at

this very moment. When did you become my ayya? I will not get up even if you stand on your head!"

By this time Ammasi's beedi had gone out. Throwing it aside, he laughed out loud. Even I burst out laughing, seeing the wicked grin on his face.

'You didn't get up till the end?' I asked, unable to suppress my curiosity.

'Adey, did you think I would get up? Let me tell you some more then.' Saying this he changed his voice.

"Elai...are you trying to act big in front of the landlord who measures out the grain to you? You don't seem to have the smallest bit of your father's loyalty. When the landlord comes, all the Pallars and Parayars stand up in respect. You youngsters don't seem to know all this."

"Yov," I said, *"I can't get up and I will not. And saying any more will not add to your stature!"*

'I got down as soon as we reached Nettiyakallu. He was still grumbling. That's all I said, and this is what happened, machan. The fellows from our street must all be gossiping about me.'

'How did the news spread so fast to the village?' I asked.

'Don't ask me! By evening itself, Chandrasekhar had told my father about it and asked him to discipline me properly. All the shouting that my father did at home, now the entire street is discussing it.'

'The women in our village cannot keep their tongues from wagging. They're saying, "When a landlord stands, is it proper for a Parayar boy to keep sitting? Why should he have such a swollen head? He's so puffed-up, his end must be near."'

When I said this, Ammasi laughed. 'Cut it out, machan...Do you know what that old Paniyaramuthu is saying? "Landlords are like gods to us. Can we survive without them? These young lads—foolish fellows. It is said that a dog never bites the hand that feeds it, but this dog insists on leaping on the whole body, fangs and all! If the landlords want to, they can easily knock all his teeth out..." When the old man said this, machan, I could not help laughing, and then he started chewing my ear off even more.'

Ammasi laughed again as he said this. I also laughed with him, and then left.

Hardly a week had gone by when there was a flurry of talk once more in the village about another misdeed of Ammasi's. But he went about his business as usual, as if nothing had happened.

So I called out to him one day and asked, 'Yeppa, now what have you gone and done?'

He immediately turned to me and said, 'Machan, tonight there is a panchayat gathering. They are going to put on trial and then hang a great murderer.'

'Never mind the panchayat, tell me what *you* did.'

'It's me they're going to try, machan, make sure you're there,' said Ammasi.

'What's the complaint against you this time? Tell me.' I was almost pleading.

'Machan, what happened was, that Chinnayya Muthukaruppan, he came and asked me to go and divert water to that Jayashankar landlord's fields.'

'Yes, I saw you, all dressed in white, carrying your

spade. The way you were dressed, I thought you were going to have the spade repaired,' I told him.

'Machan, no need to make fun of me! Ei...can't I go to work wearing white? And I was wearing the shirt that was ironed by that Muthirulan. I paid him one rupee for it.'

'Yes, yes. The shirt wasn't wrinkled at all. Now, get back to the topic.'

'When I got to Jayashankar's fields he was standing near the pump-set. I went towards him with the spade and he started talking...' Ammasi suddenly changed his voice, mimicking the way Jayashankar spoke:

"*Elai...I told Muthukaruppan from your street to find me a man to divert water to the field. No one has shown up and it's getting late.*"

"*Muthukaruppan chinnayya asked me to come—that's why I'm here.*"

"*Do you look like someone who has come to work? You look like you're going to an office! Dolt! Couldn't that idiot find anyone else? Did he have to send you?*"

"*What's it to you? You only want to divert the water, don't you? What do you care about how I'm dressed?*"

"*Elai, do you know what the time is? Look at this fellow showing up now, like a big-shot going somewhere far away!*"

"*Annachi, only you have a wrist-watch. I don't. Only you can tell the time, Annachi. I will try and buy a watch soon, Annachi. After that I will be able to tell the time.*"

I burst out laughing seeing the look on his face, but Ammasi said, 'Wait, machan, keep listening. You should have seen his face when I called him Annachi, it was black with rage.

"What did you say? Annachi? You keep saying Annachi? Who is Annachi, da? To whom am I Annachi, da? A Parayar motherfucker dares to call me Annachi?"

"Don't say whatever comes to your mouth, because then I will also start talking. It's only your reputation that will get soiled. If you don't want me, tell me to leave, that's all."

'And I turned and left, but not before I called him a swine. I don't know what he came and reported in the village, but now these people have called for a panchayat.'

'Well, you're sure to get punished today. You called the landlord a swine?!'

'You're something else, machan! You thought they were going to try me for that! No, no, it's my calling him Annachi that has become a big crime. The panchayat is assembling for that.'

As Ammasi had said, the panchayat assembled at night. The Nattamai asked, 'Elai, Ammasi, what is our caste and what is the landlord's caste? Who can address whom as Annachi? Are you not guilty of being unreasonable?'

Ammasi replied, 'We are Parayars, they are Naickers. It was I who called him Annachi. Are you having a meeting for this?' And he scratched his head, looking confused.

All the youngsters laughed loudly at this.

The headman controlled his anger and said, 'Seri, why should I waste time asking you all this? I need a straight reply. Why did you call the landlord your Annachi?'

Ammasi's reply was instant. 'Well, he is elder to me, that's why I called him my elder brother. If he was younger, I would have called him Thambi, my little brother.'

At this, the young boys laughed even more uproariously.

'This fellow is completely wild, just listen to him! Obstinate fool,' the second Nattamai said.

The headman began again, his tone grave. 'Elai, we are not assembled here to laugh at your jokes. Till today, among Pallars and Parayas, has anyone ever addressed Naickers as blood relatives? Born yesterday, and you come up with some damn fool argument? Wasn't it wrong to address him as Annachi?'

Ammasi, too, responded gravely, 'There's nothing wrong with what I said. Did I call him mama or machan, trying to create a relationship by asking for the hand of his daughter or sister? I only called him Annachi politely, respectfully—and you raise hell? What did you people do when I addressed Irulappan, the drain-cleaner, as Annachi last week? You reproached me for addressing a Kuravar as Annachi. Now you ask me why I called a Naicker Annachi! It's just what the old woman Poovathi, says, "When a donkey shits is there a difference between what it shits first and what it shits last?" Shit is shit. All men are just men.' So saying, Ammasi walked away.

And everyone watched him leave, awestruck.

Harum-scarum Saar

Kusumbukkaran means rebellious prankster, someone always involved in some mischief or the other. In Chinnakaruvelampatti village, everyone referred to Puthiyamuthu Mama, who lived in the middle street, as kusumbukkaran. His rebelliousness, which had been there from childhood, has remained till now, even though he is married and has five or six children.

He studied only up to the fifth standard. The mischief that he engaged in while in school would make for an endless list. He stood first in everything except studies. He was always planning some prank or the other, and he had four or five boys who roamed around with him as his disciples.

When he was in the second standard, he would go to the farm well to have a bath just like the elders. If water was pumped into the tank, he would bathe in the tank and return home. Once when he went to bathe like this, the water had still not been pumped in. The elders were inside the well, swimming and bathing. Puthiyamuthu alone stood on top of the well, his shorts undone. Karuvayan who was in the water, spying him, called out,

'Elai, Puthiyamuthu, if you don't know how to swim why do you come here with the elders to take a bath? You may as well bathe at the hand-pump.' Karuvayan must have been fifteen years old, studying in the ninth or tenth standard in a school in the neighbouring village.

Puthiyamuthu could not resist showing off. 'Who said I don't know how to swim?'

'Then why are you standing there? Jump in and bathe!' And Karuvayan himself dived into the water again.

Karuvayan's mouth had barely closed when Puthiyamuthu jumped into the well from above. The speed with which he leapt, everyone thought he really knew how to swim. Only when they saw him struggling in the water did they realize that the fellow was lying through his teeth. Natarajan Chithappa who was bathing there finally taught him. Thrashing and flailing, he somehow learnt to swim.

Everyone was gossiping about Puthiyamuthu in the village. 'It's not for nothing that they say the calf knows no fear! This boy who is so young has gone and jumped into well-deep water all on his own! Never seen such a mischievous fellow,' Puthiyamuthu's Periamma rambled on when she came to visit him.

'Elai, you good-for-nothing fellow, why did you go and jump into the well like that? If you didn't know how to swim you had only to say so. Lucky that people were there! Otherwise by this time you would be dead and gone, peya magane. He has made my son hang around with him, too. What for, to fall to his death like him?'

Puthiyamuthu replied, 'Ei, Periamme when I saw

everyone swimming, I also felt like it. That's why I jumped in and lied that I knew how to swim. I knew people were there, otherwise would I have jumped? Now, do you know, I can swim better than Karuvayan! Tell your hero son to come swimming with me, I'll show him!'

'Have you heard what he's saying? This fellow who just learnt swimming today is already challenging others to a race! Look at his pig-headedness!'

Puthiyamuthu's mother laughed out aloud.

'You don't bring him up properly, that's why he goes around making mischief all the time. Give him a knock or two,' his Periamma said, then got up and left.

Two or three weeks after this incident, Puthiyamuthu, with four or five other boys, was seen searching for something in the drains by candle-light. A kind of beetle emerged at night, with yellow spots on its black shell. They would catch it and, squeezing it between two fingers, knock on its head repeatedly with another finger. When they did that, the beetle would begin farting rapidly. Then they would sing:

Pitham pitham, you go and fart!
Peeru pitham, you go and fart!
Bottom of a water-pot
Tharru Purru, you go and fart!

They would catch a beetle each and roam around the streets singing this song. Those fellows who hadn't gone with them to catch beetles would follow them around, pleading with them to let them have the beetles just for some time. Puthiyamuthu led the gang. As the crowd collected, he would swell with pride, because he was the one who had pioneered this game.

Singing their song, they would sit under the streetlight and, after crushing the beetle to death, they'd examine their fingers. Where the insect had farted, the fingers would be stained black and red. Puthiyamuthu would explain that this was the same as dyeing with henna.

They persisted with this game for a week. One night, while he was eating his meal, Puthiyamuthu's mother asked him, 'Elai, the women say that you shove your hands into drains and dig out insects! Not only you, but you take other boys along with you as well.'

'So who asked them to come with me? Amma, shall I bring an insect for you, too? Look at my fingers! See how I catch them! When they fart, that spot burns and puffs up. Shall I bring one for you tomorrow, Amma?' Puthiyamuthu was quite enthusiastic.

His grandmother, who was listening to all this, said, 'Does anyone go and stick their hands into a drain ? And he studies in a school! If you keep catching insects like this your hands will get leprosy, just wait and see! Don't you have any other game to play, you rascal?'

His mother joined his grandmother in scolding him, after which he stopped playing this game.

When he was in the fifth standard, Puthiyamuthu got hold of a razor blade from somewhere. Fixing it onto a neem twig, he used it on the scalp of Rathnam who came from the south street. He did a thorough job of shaving the boy's head down to the last hair. It took some explaining, calming Rathnam's people down and convincing them that the fellow had done it in playful innocence.

'This Puthiyamuthu has no sense at all! Does anyone shave a head so that not a single hair is left? Tell him to keep his mischief at home! If he begins shaving the heads of all the other boys in the village, will anyone spare him? Is this any way to bring up a child?' shouted Vellakannu.

Puthiyamuthu's grandmother, who was listening to this, shouted back, 'Who did you say has no sense? My grandson has no sense? You, you're so old, but show me if you can fix a blade to a neem twig and use it to shave a head! Even our village barber can't do a perfect shave like this. If he could, he would ask for five or ten rupees.'

'Elai, Puthiyamuthu, how did you shave so that not a single hair was left? Bring me that razor, let me see! Where did he learn how to do this job?' The grandmother wondered at her grandson.

Puthiyamuthu brought the razor he'd fashioned to show her. 'It's very simple, Paatti. I just attached it to the twig and said I could shave a head with it. Rathnam said it was useless, I couldn't do anything with it, so I told him I would prove it by showing him. I made him sit and yanked the blade through his hair again and again. It fell in thick curls. The fellow was silent till his whole head was completely shaved, and then he went and complained to the teacher, Paatti. I picked up my bag and ran home.'

Grandmother examined the blade and the twig and said, 'You shaved his head with this thing without a single nick! Even our barber, Subbayyan, cannot shave as well as that!'

'Doesn't Subbayyan do his work under the neem tree

in our street, Paatti? I did this only after seeing how he does it,' said Puthiyamuthu.

'You must have watched him very closely! Why can't you pay the same attention to your studies, chetha paduva?' said his grandmother.

Puthiyamuthu's mother joined in, 'Elai! You just roam around playing with that razor blade, you'll cut yourself somewhere sooner or later.'

'This can't cut my finger, Amma, that's why I've attached it to a twig. I only have to grip the twig without touching the blade to start shaving. But before that, I have to wet the hair with water,' explained Puthiyamuthu.

"You're very good at all this, but see that no one from the street complains about you. Such wisdom you were born with! It can't be driven away even with slippers! Your grandfather was the same, really mischievous! Looks like you're going to beat him at it,' his grandmother laughed.

Puthiyamuthu stopped going to school after the fifth standard. When the kamma dried up, Puthiyamuthu's father tilled a portion of the bank to sow maize. When the maize corn sprouted and flocks of sparrows came to eat up the corn, Puthiyamuthu went to stand guard there. But instead of shooing away the sparrows that landed on the corn in flocks, he stared at them in amazement. After some time, he began speaking to them.

'Now look, sparrows! You're hungry, so eat quickly and leave. If my mother turns up, you'll get a good scolding and I'll get a beating. Eat up whatever you get and leave before my mother comes. Understood?'

Those who had been to the kamma, heard him and

came back laughing. They said, 'We thought he just was a mischievous fellow but he seems to be a real nut!'

Since he had stopped going to school, Puthiyamuthu now started herding goats. But actually he was more interested in catching garden lizards and killing them. Garden lizards look somewhat similar to chameleons. He would make a noose at the end of the spine of a coconut leaf, trap five or six garden lizards in no time, and kill them. Once or twice he even caught and killed snakes with the noose.

Suppukutti, who grazed goats with Puthiyamuthu, told the other boys, 'This Puthiyamuthu, he catches snakes with his bare hands! He makes the noose for garden lizards, but even snakes are caught in it. He catches venomous snakes and kills them!'

Those boys who heard about Puthiyamuthu's expertise in snaring snakes followed him and his noose around. He caught seven garden lizards and laid them out in a row after killing them. The boys were overjoyed. They roamed around with Puthiyamuthu, unconcerned about the time passing. Then, spying the tail of a garden lizard sticking out of a burrow, Puthiyamuthu silently went up close and catching hold of the tail, yanked it out. What emerged was a large snake swallowing the head of a garden lizard! All the boys ran for their lives, but Puthiyamuthu grabbed the head of the snake and began pulling it behind him. Now the other boys came up close to watch what he was doing.

'Elaika...bring three big stones, we will kill this snake. Don't think this is some harmless water-snake, it's a venomous one! It even has a hood, see that? We will die if it bites. My Paatti told me,' said Puthiyamuthu.

The boys brought some big stones. Puthiyamuthu put the snake's body on the ground and placed the stones on its middle portion and tail. Then he pressed its head down with a stick, freed his hand and smashed its head with a stone, killing it. The boys watched, spellbound. Then they buried the dead snake and returned home. As soon as he got there, Puthiyamuthu boasted to his grandmother in great detail about how he had killed the snake. Grandmother got very rattled and said, 'Elai... Don't wag your tail at snakes! Cobras are deadly—how many times must I warn you? Don't know which inauspicious hour your mother gave birth to you! Look at him, roaming around like a good-for-nothing!'

Eventually, Puthiyamuthu grew to manhood, got married and fathered four or five children, but his rebellious nature remained unchanged. It was thus that he played a prank on Lachmana Thatha who lived in the street above his. This Thatha was at least sixty years old, but even at this age he suspected his wife of unfaithfulness and kept quarrelling with her.

One day Puthiyamuthu was sleeping under the neem tree at the east end of the village. Lachmana Thatha arrived, walking with the help of a stick. Puthiyamuthu wondered how such a fellow could suspect his wife—at their age! So he purposely asked him, 'Oye, Thatha! How come you left your wife alone in the house and came here? Couldn't you bring the old woman along?'

'How can she come with me? Isn't she roaming

around enjoying herself with Mariappan? I've grown old so now she goes to work only with him,' said Lachmana Thatha.

'Like that, is it, Thatha? That's what people are saying in the streets. These are bad times. Kaalikaalam. Why not catch them red-handed one day and bring them before the panchayat, Thatha? Only then will the old woman be under your control!' Puthiyamuthu suggested seriously.

Thatha's spirits soared as he said, 'Yes, I'm also thinking of that. But I haven't been able to catch them together even once. And my eyes are weak, can't see after dark—that's convenient for her. But I'm sure I'll catch them somehow.'

'Idiot! Can't even see properly!' Puthiyamuthu muttered to himself. 'Isn't it better for you to drink the kanji that you get and curl up on the verandah, instead of suspecting that innocent old woman?'

Four or five days later Puthiyamuthu turned up at Lachmana Thatha's, and blabbed whatever came to his mind.

'Thatha, you know what's happening? That fellow Mariappan and your old woman are meeting daily at the pump-set in Poochi Naicker's field. The boys from our street have seen them. If you go there in the evening, you can catch them red-handed!'

'Is that so? Now what did I say? No one believed me when I said that, now they themselves have seen it. You see what kind of character that old woman is? I'll go there tomorrow evening, catch hold of the bitch red-handed, make her life miserable. If I don't catch her now, I'll hang myself, said Thatha, all worked up and huffing and puffing with the effort.

Seeing him so agitated, Puthiyamuthu laughed to himself and left. The next day he called four or five youngsters together and went to Poochi Naicker's pump-set to lie in wait for Thatha.

When darkness fell, Lachmana Thatha crept up, quiet as a cat, supporting himself with his stick. But as he couldn't see properly, he fell into a disused well on the way. Hearing his cries for help, Puthiyamuthu and the boys ran to his rescue.

News spread fast, and by the time Thatha was brought home a big crowd had collected. It was only then that his old woman, who had gone to sift paddy on the west side of the village, returned home. As soon as she arrived, she asked him in a broken voice, 'Why did you go to the pump-set at this hour of the night? Why couldn't you curl up at home after drinking your kanji.'

Puthiyamuthu said, 'He went there in search of you, Paatti.'

'I went to sift paddy on the west side of the village—why did he go to the pump-set looking for me? It was lucky that you people were also there otherwise he would be a corpse! He can't see a thing! Why can't he just curl up in some corner instead of straining himself?' The old grandmother went on and on in this vein.

'Oh, he went looking for you only to catch you and Mariappan together, to drag you both to the panchayat,' said Puthiyamuthu.

When she heard this, the old woman's anger knew

no bounds. She picked up the broom that she had taken to sweep the paddy with and set about beating the old man with it, cursing loudly as the blows landed on him. 'Why did you rescue this rotten fellow from the well? You should have left him there to die! We could have lived with some dignity if he were buried for good.'

Stopping her, Puthiyamuthu said, 'Seri, seri, leave it, Paatti. Let's see if he becomes wiser after this.'

When he heard this the old man said, 'Elai, Puthiyamuthu, like Andi who blew the conch that was just lying around and spoiled everything, are you watching the fun after provoking me? You'll never make good! But why blame you? I should give myself a good thrashing. I listened to you and got beaten up with a broom. Can I live after being beaten up by a woman? I'll hang myself tonight!'

'Seri, if you are a real man, hang yourself, I'll go and dig a grave for you. But be sure you do hang yourself or our efforts will go waste! You're worthless. Didn't you think it wrong to suspect an innocent old woman? All you feel bad about is getting a beating from her!' Everyone sniggered when they heard this.

'Elai, don't you play your pranks on me, doi! I trusted you like a fool who trusts a clay horse to cross the river! You wretch!'

But Puthiyamuthu just laughed and left the scene.

The next afternoon Puthiyamuthu came and sat in the chavady. Thoplan, who was already there, berated him, 'Ei, Mama, you shouldn't make so much mischief. Didn't you get that poor, half-blind old man to fall into the well and then enjoy the sight? You didn't even think of his age!'

'Ei, did I invite him there? If he's so stupid that he falls into a well, what can *I* do? You call him an old man, but was he behaving like one? Why should he be so pigheaded at this age?' asked Puthiyamuthu.

'That's true, Mama, but what if he had got himself hurt or killed?'

'We wouldn't have let it go that far—didn't we keep an eye on him? But the old man went and fell before we could reach him.'

'Seri. And didn't you conduct an operation on a goat last week? Is it alive or dead?' asked Thoplan.

'Ei, why ask such questions? Has any goat that I laid my hands on ever died? Who do you think I am?' countered Puthiyamuthu, bristling with pride.

'Well, have you studied to be a doctor? Doing surgery as you please! How did you do it, Mama? It's amazing!'

'What's amazing about it? The goat had a tumour-like swelling in its belly. I thought I would slit it to squeeze out the pus, then apply some medicine and bandage it. But when I opened it up it was not a tumour or anything like that. When I cut through the skin to have a look, it was nothing but intestines bulging out.'

'So what did you do then?'

'I had to think quickly, what else? I immediately pushed the intestines back in and stitched up the skin.'

'What did you stitch it with?'

'Don't we have lines for the fishing rod? I looped that through a needle and sewed it up.'

'How did you get the needle through the skin, Mama?'

'It was tough. But I pushed the thick end, slowly got it through and stitched it like that. Then I ground some medicinal leaves in neem oil and applied the paste to the wound till it healed. The goat is quite active now.'

'You really are a rare individual, Mama. People say you were like this from childhood!'

'Looks like you want to keep me here forever. Seri, da! Ramasami Ayya has asked me to do some paddy transplanting and ridge-levelling work in his fields tomorrow. I have to find four more boys to do the work, so I have no more time for chatting.' Saying this, Puthiyamuthu got up and left.

Early next morning he went about the paddy-transplanting and ridge-levelling work, then went to Ramasami Ayya's house in the evening to collect his wages.

When he saw Puthiyamuthu, Ramasami Ayya asked, 'Ennale, have you come to get your wages? Go and feed the cattle in the cowshed first, then come back.'

Puthiyamuthu did as he was told and returned.

'Ennale, have you fed the cattle? Seri, now go and get some money from Amma and buy five kilos of paruthikottai and two kilos of kambu—the milch cows need it.'

Though he was seething with anger, Puthiyamuthu controlled himself. He went and did all the shopping. When he came back, Ramasami Ayya said, 'Elai, I sent two spades to the carpenter, Thangavelu, to fix the handles. See if he has finished with them.'

Puthiyamuthu's anger knew no bounds, but still he kept himself in check and brought the spades back. This set the landlord thinking, 'Oh, have you brought them? What shall we do now?'

Puthiyamuthu ground his teeth and spat out, 'Now? Go, bring your wife here—we'll take turns bedding her.'

Ramasami looked absolutely stricken, as if he had seen a ghost.

Chilli Powder

Every day, something or other would be said about Gangamma in the village. Even if it was only an infant crying, it was enough to say that Gangamma was on her way and it would immediately shut up.

Gangamma possessed immense wealth in the form of fields and orchards. Though she had an ugly figure, with a paunch like a swollen toad stuck to a coconut leaf, Balarama Naicker's son, Jagannatha Naicker, tied the knot with her with an eye on her wealth. It seems she remained barren for many years after the marriage. The villagers used to say that her body was stuffed with so much fat that she couldn't have given birth to a single child. But after ten or twelve years had passed, Gangamma became pregnant all of a sudden, and delivered a baby girl. After the child attained puberty she was married off in some distant town. Since then Gangamma had been living all alone in her house. She had no siblings, and her parents had died long back. She looked after the farm and after the harvest, sent off whatever she got to her daughter's house in town. The fine daughter, too, would pay her a visit twice a year and gather up whatever rice, grains or green beans she could lay her hands on and cart them off.

They say Gangamma's house looked like a palatial bungalow with a ground floor and a first floor. People wondered how she could live all alone in such a huge house. It had been built in the time of her grandfather, Sivarama Naicker. Echakkimuthu's family, who lived in the colony, did all the domestic work in and around the house, as well as the farm labour in the fields and plantations. Echakki's son, Karuthapandi, was dead scared of Gangamma. He tried everything he could to escape the sight of her, but Gangamma forced him to stay by her side, saying he couldn't work anywhere else without first repaying the loan his father had taken from her.

Anyone would hold their breath at the sight of Gangamma, she was such a massive figure. Her hands and legs were as huge as an elephant's. Still, lugging this huge body along, she would tirelessly do a round of all her fields and orchards regularly. There must have been at least fifty or sixty acres of land to her name, and all of it was fertile, where one could sow and reap gold. She didn't leave an inch of space uncultivated. She supervised everything; even hired labour with an eagle eye.

Everyone in the colony was scared of Gangamma, but Pachayamma wasn't the least bit in awe of her. She was so brazen that she would cut grass only in Gangamma's fields. Since no one else dared to go there, it was good hunting for her. She would cut the thick grass, bundle it up and carry it away without a trace of fear. That wasn't all. As if she hadn't already done the unthinkable, she then went around the streets bragging about what she had done.

One time, Pachayamma, who had come to the tap to collect water, boasted, 'Today I went to Gangamma's mango orchard to cut the grass. You should see that grass—how thick it grows! I cut so much that when I bundled it up and tried to lift it, I found I couldn't do it alone. I rolled up my munthanai and placed it on my head, looking here and there, thinking if someone came along I would ask them to help me lift the bundle. But there wasn't a crow or sparrow in sight. It was getting late. I thought, maybe I should leave some grass behind and carry the rest, but I couldn't bring myself to do that. I decided to wait for some more time, plucked two mangoes from the tree nearby, sliced them with my sickle and started eating them. I was hungry. Though they belonged to that wicked woman, I must admit... what fruits they were! Dripping with honey! Not the least bit sour. Even as I was enjoying them, Gangamma herself appeared. I hid the mangoes in my sari and asked her to help me lift the bundle of grass. That woman got so furious she was swaying like an elephant calf gone mad! Don't know from where I got the courage, I held my breath, heaved the bundle onto my head and half walking, half running, rushed back here.'

'Ei, don't exaggerate! As if she would have let you go,' said Parvatham, who was standing nearby.

'What can she do, eh? She can't touch a hair on my head. If she runs ten feet, this Pachayamma can run eighteen!' And having said enough, she picked up her pot and proceeded to collect some water.

After two or three days Pachayamma, along with two other women, went to Gangamma's fields again to cut grass. While they were busy, Gangamma crept up on them. Moving like a cat, she quietly returned to her house and came back with chilli powder rolled in a sheet of paper. It suited her that the field was near her house. She came right up to the ridge where Pachayamma was cutting grass and said, 'You thieving wretch, is it because you have no other place to go to that you come here and slit my throat? Your own colony women say that you are shameless! Looks like they're right. Everyone else does a detour when they come upon Gangamma's fields—but you, you have to show off, eh?' Hardly had she finished saying this than she threw the chilli powder into Pachayamma's eyes.

As soon as the chilli hit her eyes, Pachayamma went wild with rage. Wiping her burning eyes with the end of her munthanai she began shouting, 'Chi, can you be called a woman? Throwing chilli powder in my eyes just for cutting grass that grows on its own? Is there such a harvest of fruits and vegetables here that we will come and steal them? Look at her face, swollen like a huge gourd! And look at the shameless widow's belly, bulging as if she is perpetually ten months pregnant! Your husband popped off after just one child because of your character, di!'

Still hurling abuses, she bundled up the grass and called out to the two women who had accompanied her, 'Better gather up your grass quickly. Oh, my eyes! Whore-widow! May you be taken around like a corpse in procession! I can't open my eyes at all! May you have a leper's hands! Look at the dead bitch standing there like a fat pot of grain.' So saying, Pachayamma left, and the other women ran back with her, glad to have got off lightly.

Gangamma wasn't keeping mum either. She matched abuse for abuse. Even after she left her fields Pachayamma continued her haranguing, 'Don't get a swollen head just because you threw chilli powder into my eyes today! Slut! Evil eye! Has a fitting name, too... Gangamma Nolliyamma...not even a shitting dog will look up when you pass...Look at her...swinging her hair like a rat's tail!'

This incident was the only topic of discussion that day in the streets. Everyone had a different version.

'Knowing that woman so well, why did these women go there to cut grass? Why such arrogance?'

'But how could she be so crafty? She took the trouble to go home and bring the chilli powder to throw into Pachayamma's eyes! What if she had gone blind? If this is what she does just for cutting grass, what will she do if someone touches her harvest? She wouldn't hesitate to kill!'

'And where else can we go and cut grass if not in the fields and orchards of landowners? Where else do we go for grass to feed the cattle we survive on? As if she owns some special kind of fields that no one else in the world has!'

'Ei, it's not right to speak about her like this. It's this Pachayamma who has developed such a swollen head that she keeps going only to that woman's fields. Like a fat crab that can't stay in its hole. No one else goes to her fields—why should Pachayamma alone go there as if she is the governor's wife?'

After this, everyone began referring to Gangamma as molagappodi—chilli powder. The woman would get furious at just a mention of the word, but Pachayamma and the other women enjoyed themselves by repeatedly saying 'molagappodi' in her presence.

It was thus that one day Pachayamma and four or five women were returning home after working in the mustard fields, and seeing Gangamma approaching from a distance, Pachayamma said provocatively, 'Heard that a chilli powder machine has come to our village, too. The wife of that teacher who lives in the street beyond us, she isn't grinding chilli paste any more—she's using chilli powder, just like the landowners do.'

'Is that so, mathini. Must be so convenient to store chilli powder like that. We can use it to cook and also to throw into people's eyes.'

Gangamma drew abreast of the women just as Chittamma finished speaking. Walking a few steps ahead of them, she began yelling furiously, 'Yendi, stinking whore-widow! How dare you talk like this? She's so poor she has next to nothing to wear, but look how the donkey speaks! Brazen bitch!'

When she heard this, Pachayamma's anger exploded and she made as if to strike Gangamma with her vessel of koozh. The other women also joined in. Trapped, Gangamma did not stop to reply. She took to her heels, huffing and puffing all the way.

Two weeks later, ten or twelve women who had gone to cut weeds near the forest in the upper reaches of the village were returning home after finding there was no work for them. Pachayamma said, 'No work, no wages! Don't know what I'm going to cook a meal with today. What kind of life is this! You get kanji only if you work! Otherwise, you just drink some water and go to sleep.'

'Ei...what's your problem? Your man would have earned enough when he returns...'

'Be quiet! Are you talking about that useless fellow? For two whole months he was without work. Then last month he left, saying there is well-digging work somewhere and he has to stay there. I don't know whether he'll stay and finish the work or leave it halfway and come back. His heart is not in his work and you are counting on him?' Pachayamma plucked some full-grown pods from the cotton plants growing there and tucked them into her waist. Seeing her, the other women followed suit and in no time, each had collected a nice pile of pods. On the way they didn't hesitate to lay their hands on Gangamma's plantation, too. As if on cue, Gangamma made her appearance right then. Seeing Pachayamma, she swore she would teach the women a lesson one way or another, and hurried back to her house.

Just then, a police inspector and two policemen came to Gangamma's street on work. She saw them and immediately took them to her plantation. The inspector was their own man—he used to stay in Gangamma's elder brother Chinnachami Naicker's house, on the top floor. Gangamma lost no time in using this connection.

Pachayamma and the other women, who were still plucking the cotton pods, were taken aback when Gangamma suddenly returned with the policemen. Immediately, they lifted their bundles and started running for it. But even as she ran, Pachayamma said, 'See what that molagappodi has done? Brought policemen with her! Done it only to create problems for us. Everyone listens to money.'

'Ei...keep quiet, Akka. For once, don't spoil everything by talking too much! Compromise, think of how to get home now. See, finally we got caught today!' complained Madathi.

'How long have you been making a living stealing from someone else's fields?' demanded one of the policemen. 'Everyone, drop the pods and come with us to the station!'

Pachayamma retorted, 'Why should we? All this cotton is not from this plantation only—we have picked most of it from what was lying around in the wasteland to the west. We only picked this much from here.' Saying this, she dumped the pods from her waist-band on the ground.

'Open up all the bundles! Let's see if they are from the wasteland or not,' demanded Gangamma.

Since the policemen also insisted, all the bundles were opened up and the pods heaped on the ground. Finding that they were good quality cotton, the policeman said,

Chilli Powder

'Does this look like cotton from the wasteland? How will the farmers make a profit if you steal like this? To the station, everyone!' And so all the women were loaded onto Gangamma's tractor and taken to the police station.

On the way, each one started blaming or swearing at the other. Pachayamma finally made them all keep quiet.

'Why are you quarrelling with each other now? Are they going to cut our heads off at the station? Take it easy, women! As for me, I'm dying to pee.'

As she finished, Veerayi said, 'Isn't it bad enough that we have been caught stealing like this? This has never happened before, we have never been taken to the police station. We are in this mess because of you. Don't be so shameless.'

'Ei...what's shameful about this? Are we stealing so we can build tiled houses for ourselves? Are we going to make jewellery for our necks and ears? We steal because that is the only way we will not starve—even though we need only a little bit of kanji. Tell me, with prices so high, can we afford to have our fill of kanji with the wages we get? We don't have a single coin on us today. Even when there is work and we get paid, we can have only broken-rice kanji and rasam. Today I thought I would sell the cotton and buy some dried fish for a curry, but that sinner's daughter came and spoiled it all.' Pachayamma turned her attention to the policeman. 'Ayya, just let me get down for a second. I'll pee and come running back.'

'We can't let you down anywhere, you'll get down only at the station. Now keep your mouth shut,' said the policeman.

'Who is this fellow, talking to us as if he's telling schoolchildren to shut their mouths? Have our mouths been open till now?' Pachayamma laughed as she said this. All the other women began laughing too, and were in high spirits now, taunting and mimicking each other till they reached the station.

Old woman Kalathi was disapproving, 'How can one sit in this thing and travel? Up-down, up-down, it keeps tossing us up and down. What kind of stupid vehicle is this? And look at these women, laughing as if they are on their way to some holy festival. Keep quiet, you!'

Pachayamma said in reply, 'You keep quiet, Periamma. The way this vehicle is swaying, I'm unable to control my bladder. These fellows won't even let us pee. If it takes any longer, I will be forced to squat right here, it's getting so bad!'

When they reached the station, the policemen ordered them to get down. As soon as she did, Pachayamma quickly lifted her clothes and peed right there, standing up. The other women, too, did the same. Seeing this the policemen grumbled, 'Chi, arrogant donkeys! They'll make the whole station stink!'

Pachayamma said, 'Ayya, one can hold back one's anger, but not one's piss. That's why we asked you to let us down on the way. It's you who said we could pee only after reaching the station,' she laughed.

'Seri, seri, hurry up, it's getting late.'

'Only after peeing could we stand straight,' saying this Pachayamma started walking away. The other women, too, followed her. Seeing this, one of the policeman

Chilli Powder

shouted, 'Ei...Ei...where are you off to? Come back here and pay ten rupees fine per head!'

'What do you mean by shouting ei and oi? Are you our husbands to call us "ei"? We picked the cotton with great difficulty, to sell. But this fellow asked us to drop the pods there itself and now you're asking us to pay ten rupees fine? What a joke! We can't even buy some broken rice to make kanji at home, and he demands ten rupees! Ten rupees! Who are you trying to fool? We don't have a single coin to buy even a small packet of snuff and you know that.'

'We're not interested in all that. You can leave here only after paying the fine,' the policeman replied.

'This is too much! Like the story of the blind man who was told to have a king's vision! What will we pay the fine with? Seri, if you don't want us to leave, we won't. We will all stay here, you give us food for the night. In the morning we will go to work, come back in the evening and pay the fine. Ei, come on, women, we'll just sit here.' Pachayamma sat right down and all the other women sat down with her. Old woman Kalathi spread out her munthanai and curled up.

Just then, the inspector came up on his bike. The two policemen immediately sprang into action, rushed to the women and ordered them to stand up. To this, Pachayamma said, 'Look at them, rushing here and there just at the sound of the motor! These fellows who shit at the sight of the inspector, you should see them at home, twirling their moustaches, acting like heroes in front of their wives.'

'Ei, shut up, mathini. Stop blowing your trumpet. When an officer shows up, they all hang on to his balls,' said Aarayi.

The inspector stopped his bike, looked at everyone without getting down, and brayed like a donkey. 'I am letting you go this time! But if you do this again, I'll put all of you in the lock-up...now, get out!'

All of them rushed home, but by this time the news had spread through the village and everyone was discussing it.

'Enna? Are you back after visiting the station? How come they released you so quickly? How much did you pay?' asked Paniyaramuthu.

'No fine, Mama. They just took us there, then released us,' replied Pachayamma.

But everyone was saying all sorts of things in the street. 'Yes, yes, let them. Let them talk. It was all that molagappodi's handiwork. She must have thought they would take us to the station and molest us. As it turned out, it was like waiting for the elephant to fart and then hearing only a bubble burst!' Pachayamma said angrily.

By this time her husband, who had gone on well-digging work, came back home. When he heard that Pachayamma had been at the police station, he started yelling at her. 'Etha, do you have any brains? If you have to steal, steal without getting caught. You've been to the station and back for the sake of some stupid cotton. Idiot woman!'

'Ei...don't speak like a fool, machan. The village people are gossiping without knowing a thing, and you also join in! Show me one woman in the street who has not stolen something. You said you're going to work, but here you are.'

'I know you will only blame me, useless woman. Aren't you ashamed, going to the station? Your whole family is a pack of thieves!'

Pachayamma silenced her husband at once, 'Yes, I went to the station and came back. What's wrong with that? Tell me something: has any woman who worked in the fields arrived at our village in such style, in a vehicle? Didn't we come here in Gangamma's own vehicle? The station isn't so far from our village, is it?'

'Not satisfied with stealing, she's brazen as well! You will end up with just your tongue left, atha. It's right what they say, whether your mouth is stitched up or locked up, you can't help babbling!'

'Seri, I have no time to waste talking to you. What do you know? These days, if we don't speak up, they'll come and fart right in our faces, aama.'

Saying this, she walked towards Veluchami's shop, hoping to get some ragi flour from him on credit to cook some kali.

Rich Girl

'Mothalali is going on shouting, "Don't come to work with the baby!" New-born child, still has my milk on its tongue. How can I leave it behind?'

The roosters were crowing at daybreak, when Kaliyamma, having mixed some cow dung in water, began sprinkling it vigorously in front of the door.

'When I say, "It's only a baby, ayya, how can I leave it and come?" he says unkindly, "Ask your elder daughter to take care of it, what great thing is she going to achieve by studying?"'

Saying this she gathered up her pots and ran towards the street tap to collect water.

'Don't know who laid pipes in street after street and brought the water here like this. Kind soul...otherwise we'd be putting a bucket into the well and going heave, heave, heave for water.'

With one mud pot on her head and another at her waist, Kaliyamma doubled back home as fast as she could.

'How can we go to work like this? Where do I leave the baby? Shall we take Ramayi along to carry it, like mothalali says?'

Her husband, Muthukaruppan, replied, 'Let Ramayi study. Or let her carry the baby to school. She can look after it and also study, can't she?'

'That's true. Ramayi, you take care of the baby. When they serve the noon meal, give some to your brother as well. Keep this ten-paisa coin in any case. If he cries, buy him a biscuit or something. Watch over him carefully. Your father and I will come back in the evening. Now drink up the koozh and go to school, it's getting late for us.'

Eight-year-old Ramayi did not like going to school at all. 'Amma, why can't I carry him and come with you to mothalali's house? I will look after him there. Or I'll stay home and take care of him. I'll make him sleep and then go with Pechiyamma to the field to pick the fallen paddy, then to the kamma to catch fish and come back home. They say they are reaping Gopalasamy Ayya's field today.'

Muthukaruppan heard what Ramayi had to say and replied, 'Don't even go near the kamma with the baby! It's overflowing. Before you know it, you will be neck deep in it. If you listen to your mother and go to school, you and your brother will at least get four mouthfuls of gruel! Look how she talks! I'm warning you, watch it or you'll die from my thrashing!'

Ramayi bowed her head at the severity of her father's tone. Gulping down the koozh, hoisting her brother Karuppasami onto her waist, carrying the food-plate in her hand and not forgetting to tuck the ten-paisa coin her mother had given her into her waist-band, Ramayi left for school. And Kaliyamma and Muthukaruppan went to work to their mothalali's house.

Those who left at sunrise returned only after darkness had fallen. After toiling at mothalali's house and in his fields for the whole year, they came home daily with only the stale, leftover rice from his house and two sacks of paddy at harvest time as wages.

Ramayi was their eldest child. Karuppasami came next. After Ramayi was born, Kaliyamma had miscarriages for eight years before Karuppasami was born.

After reaching school, Ramayi seated her brother beside her on the floor and began reciting the one and two-times tables that her teacher was chanting. Suddenly, Cheeniyamma, who was sitting next to her, stood up, saying, 'Ethaa, Ramayi, your brother is shitting! Saar, Ramayi's brother is shitting!'

The teacher immediately pinched his nose and said, 'Babies should not be brought to school. Take him outside right now!'

Chided, Ramayi carried her brother outside and, setting him down on the ground, covered the shit on the ground with some sand.

'Why did you bring the baby here today?' the teacher asked angrily.

Ramayi, trembling with fear, said, 'My father and mother have gone to work. Our mothalali warned them not to bring the baby there. That's why my mother asked me to take him instead.'

'So, do you have to come here and fill the school with the foul smell of his shit? Stupid donkey! Take him away, go home at once!' shouted the teacher as he led the other children out and sat under a tree.

Ramayi picked up a scrap of paper from the floor to wipe her brother's bottom with, hoisted him onto her waist once again, picked up her plate and left. On the way, she found children of her own community playing at the kamma. Ramayi joined them. Setting her brother down on the ground, she jumped into the kamma with her same-street friend, Pechiyamma, and started swimming, all the time facing the bank and keeping an eye on her brother from the water. It was only after seven or eight years that there was so much water in the kamma. Someone had removed the plank from the dyke. Some were catching fish. The streets were overflowing with fish—jalebi, kenda and suchlike were as big as a man's arms or legs, having grown to the size of sea-fish.

On the banks of the kamma that day, washermen got busy with the clothes and little children were busy swimming. The men who came to bathe their cattle were doing so a little farther away. Where the water was still, young folk were sitting with fishing rods, while younger ones were standing on guard looking out for the kamma watchman. If the contractor came along, he wouldn't allow anyone to continue fishing. Not only that, he would confiscate the fish that had been caught and break their fishing rods.

The moment Ramayi spied her father coming to the kamma to wash the bullocks, she got out of the water quickly and, tying her skirt, picked up her brother once again.

Seeing her, Muthukaruppan shouted, 'I send you to school and here you are, playing! Good-for-nothing girl, a few slaps and you'll come to your senses!' Leaving the bullocks to enter the water he began chasing Ramayi.

Not wanting to be caught by him, and not letting go of the plate still in her hands either, Ramayi ran straight towards her school.

When he saw this, Muthu stopped running, got into the water and began washing the bullocks. Mothalali had asked him to bathe them and tie them up, before fetching the cow and the buffalo for their wash, and then to take them to the milking-shed. But even as he was busy with one of them, the other one swam out to the middle of the kamma.

'How far does he think he can go? He will have to swim back. Just look at his arrogance! All the other bullocks are on this side, but this one has to swim alone to the very middle of the kamma.'

Still looking at the bullock that had swum away, Muthu asked the other men to tether it as soon as it reached the bank, and proceeded in the direction of mothalali's house to fetch the other cow and buffalo.

'Ennale, you could have brought the bullocks back and yoked them before taking the cow and buffalo for their wash and continued in the same direction to milk them,' said mothalali.

'I have tied one bullock to the banyan tree near the kamma, sami. The other one swam to the middle of the water while I was busy. I have asked the people there to catch him and tie him up,' Muthu told his mothalali.

'You lazy fool! You left a bullock that costs two-three thousand rupees just like that in the water? Have you any sense? If something happens to it, consider yourself skinned! Go back this instant and bring the bullock to the bank, you dog!'

Muthu ran at once towards the kamma.

The bullock was still in the water. Losing no time, Muthu jumped in and swam towards him, pulling him back towards the bank. But the bullock swam away. Muthu started following him, but took one look at the bank from the middle of the kamma and, suddenly, his mind flipped. The kamma was as full as an ocean. Awe-struck, Muthu hesitated, wondering how to cross so much water and reach the bank. Suddenly, his hands waving frantically towards the bank, he went down.

The people on the bank immediately threw the threshing plank into the water in order to save him, but by that time he had come up and gone down thrice before finally drowning.

In no time, the bank was crowded with people. They began searching the water with planks and palm-tree logs to at least retrieve Muthu's body.

As soon as school was over, Ramayi picked up her brother and started for home. Seeing the crowd on the banks of the kamma, she ran towards it. She saw Pechiyamma standing there. 'Pechi, why is there such a crowd here today?' she asked, lowering her brother to the ground.

'They are looking for your father only, stupid! He seems to have gone to the middle of the kamma and disappeared. They're all searching for him,' replied Pechiyamma.

'My father knows how to swim, he can swim in any kind of water,' said Ramayi, rolling her eyes and shaking her head. She picked up her brother and walked towards the dyke. There, seeing her mother and four or five other women wailing and screaming, she ran towards Kaliyamma. As soon as she saw her children, Kaliyamma began wailing even more loudly.

'It is already five o'clock, the body is not yet found. There is so much water—where does one search for it in this? And more water is gushing in from the dyke. At this rate we don't know where it will take the body and bury it...'

Even as people were saying all this, the body was found, placed on a plank and brought to the bank. When it arrived, all the people assembled there started wailing, raising a huge uproar. People from all over came running to the kamma. The body was moved to the banyan tree and propped up against it.

Kaliyamma, along with her children, ran and fell against it, crying most piteously, her sobs resounding across the kamma-bank and the fields.

'I have been living here for many, many years but have never seen such an untimely death before.'

'A curse on that mothalali fellow! For a mere bullock he sent this man to his death. Can he ever prosper? Will his family prosper?'

'If you lose a bullock you can buy another. If a man is lost, can we buy another? He killed him for no reason at all!'

'Why blame mothalali? Whenever the kamma is full, she demands a sacrifice. This time it was Muthu's turn.'

'He must have got a real fright, seeing himself surrounded by so much water. Was it so difficult for him to cross over? He could have swum back to the bank.'

'Wonder if some spirit possessed him—the fellow couldn't have been so frightened otherwise.'

'There's a whirlpool right there in the middle of the kamma. If you get caught in it not even an able swimmer can escape. I think this Muthu got trapped in that.'

'Did mothalali come and have a look?'

'How can he come if a mere Chakkiliyar dies? When people went and told him he just said the bullock could have come back on its own, why did this madman take such a risk and get himself killed?'

Talking among themselves, the Chakkiliyars took the body to the cremation ground and returned to their respective huts after cremating it.

After this, Ramayi stopped going to school and went with her mother to work in mothalali's house. She looked after the child and did all the menial household jobs there.

One day, after finishing her work, Ramayi came home, took her brother Karuppasami to the street and was playing under the streetlight when Pechiyamma turned up, too.

'Etha, Pechi, we are rich now, did you know?' Ramayi said to her friend happily. 'Mothalali gave us one hundred rupees for my father's death. My mother now has a hundred rupees, did you know?' Overwhelmed with happiness, Ramayi licked the piece of jaggery in her hand.

'Dying by drowning gets you one hundred rupees?' Pechiyamma found this difficult to digest.

'No, no, nothing like that, atha. You know nothing! Only if you drown while washing mothalali's bullocks will he give you one hundred rupees.'

So saying, Ramayi took another small bite of the jaggery, then gave the rest to Pechiyamma.

Those Days

'That's how it was in those days, but it can't be the same today, can it? No.' Every now and then Masanam Thatha asked this question and provided the answer himself.

'Those days, if landlords came upon us street fellows while we were smoking, we would quickly hide the beedis and stand up respectfully. But now? Today's chaps light up their beedis only when landlords approach! And after lighting up, they hold their heads high and blow out the smoke, puff after puff.' While saying this, Thatha bent his right leg slightly to one side, as he mimicked smoking and blowing out the smoke, a mischievous smile on his face.

He came to Marimuthu's tailoring shop, picked up the stool lying there and sat on it. 'Elay, Mari!' he called out, 'In those days did anyone tailor clothes like this? All the men were doing village work. But now, no one does that. That's how it was those days. Who goes now?'

'What village work, Mama?' Marimuthu was curious.

'All our people used to toil for upper-caste people only. If cattle died in their street, our men had to carry the corpses and bury them. If someone died in their homes, our fellows went from village to village informing them of the death. We also had to beat the drums in the houses where someone had died. We had to carry the dead body and cremate it.

'Those days, if they beat the drums for one whole day, they would get one rupee for it. Now? They are so obstinate that they will not beat the drums anymore. "Would we allow anyone to cheat us the way they did in those days? We will not, le!"'

'We even used to drink koozh from their hands, le, Mama?'

'Aamama! They would distribute koozh after worshipping their god and we would go to them shamelessly, like dogs, with pots and pans to collect the koozh that they poured into them. That's how it was, those days. And now? No one wants their koozh. They'll be waiting there with plenty of koozh, but who wants it now? No one.'

'Did you hear something else? That Paniyaramuthu, it seems he went for a shave after taking the landlord's permission, but got a bit late going back. So the landlord caught him.'

'And what did he do then?'

'The landlord questioned him about it.

"*Elay! What took you so long? Didn't you know you had to rush back?*"

"*I got a bit delayed at the shop,*" *he replied.*

"*Got delayed at the shop? You went for a shave, le?*"

"*Aama! The barber's shop was crowded, that's why I got late.*"

"What! You went to the barber's shop for a shave? Ei! Why couldn't you just go to the barber on your street and get shaved under the neem tree, as usual?"

"I thought I should try the shop and so I went to the one opposite the Sarada Hotel."

"What! That's the shop I go to myself! You went and sat on the same chair as me?"

"Ei! So what if I did? I also pay cash. If you pay cash, you can sit. If I pay cash, I can sit. I paid cash, so I sat down.'"

Masanam, who was narrating all this with the appropriate body movements, continued with a laugh, 'That's how it was, in those days. Would it happen now? If anyone says anything like that now, our fellows answer back, word for word. Aama.'

Masanam removed the towel from his shoulder, shook it out, put it back, got up and left. While walking he said to himself, 'Those days, our people lived a life that was worse than dogs. Now, we're also educated and move around in white clothes. People who sleep on mud floors, will they sleep on them forever? One day, will they not roll onto a mat? They will. When we begin to sleep on mats, it is they who get heartburn.'

During election time, when door to door campaigning was on, Masanam Thatha again chipped in with his comments.

'Those days, one could not vote secretly against a symbol and drop it in the box. The white man was ruling then. Village people would be herded together and the candidates would be asked to stand in front of them, and those who were going to vote for one of them would be asked to raise their hands. The raised hands would be counted. Then those who wanted to vote for the other would be asked to raise their hands. These would also be counted. The person who got the maximum raised hands would win. Four policemen would be standing there.

'What happens now? If they want votes, whether mothalali or mothaliyar, they come to our doorstep looking for us. Then they act as if there is unity between them and us. When I see these fellows roaming around like beggars, I really feel like laughing!'

Velusami, who was listening to Masanam Thatha, said, 'Those days you were not educated, that's why they asked you to raise your hands. Now, so many are educated, le? So we vote like this now.'

'Poda, useless fellow! Some education! At least we knew who we were voting for. Now, who sees their faces? Stamp here, stamp there, that's what they tell everyone. Those who vote look for the symbol and vote, that's all. If you ask me, the white man's rule was better. Were the farmers of those days like the ones today? If you had a one-rupee coin you could get a sackful of things. Can you get that now? No, you cannot.'

'You always talk about those days. Try to remember what happened last week, then you'll know whether it was "those days" or "these days",' said Velusami.

Last Saturday the landlord Maruthappan was tied to the fig tree at the edge of the village. There was such a huge crowd there that if a mustard seed had dropped from above it would not have touched the ground. Men and women were talking animatedly. Masanam Thatha was also in the crowd.

'Are you so arrogant that you dare to grab the hand of a girl from our street?' hissed Lokamma. 'And abuse her while she cries for mercy again and again! People like you should be thrown into a lime kiln to roast. Palavatrappayal!'

Masanam Thatha also raised his voice, 'It was only in those days that we remained quiet! You would harass our girls as you pleased, terrify them the moment you set eyes on them. Did you think things were still the same when you laid hands on her? We will hack you to pieces! Aama!'

'Patience, Thatha! People from their street are on their way here, we will talk to them.'

'Why should I be patient? This is the arrogance of their caste. They think we are stupid, just like in those days. That was then. Now, we will count the bones in their bodies. Aama!'

Ten or twenty people from Maruthappan mothalali's street arrived. The elder among them said, 'What has happened has happened. What can we do? Whatever you ask, we are ready to do.'

Masanam spoke up before anyone else could. 'You better give the thali to him and ask him to tie it around the girl's neck. Didn't he take her, hidden from everyone's view? Now, let him tie the knot and take her home as his wife with the full knowledge of the people.'

While everyone cried out that this was the right thing to do, a man from Maruthappa's street spoke. 'How can that be? Look at your caste and look at ours. What is your status and what is ours? Is this a workable solution? Take five or ten thousand and untie him.'

Masanam Thatha shouted back, 'So, only now you think about caste and status and all that? He didn't think about caste when he touched her! You think we are stupid? Call that girl here. Tie the knot, you thattuvanippayale.'

But when the girl came, she spoke up. 'I don't want to live as a wife with this animal. I don't want him to tie the knot with me.'

'Ha! The girl herself is saying so, why are you complicating things? Just let the matter rest!' Maruthappan's people spoke on his behalf.

'Rest? Would you let it rest if the fellows from our street did the same to girls from your street? Do only *you* have shame and honour? We people go about naked, shamelessly?'

'Okay, okay, take ten thousand rupees and let him go.'

'Ten thousand is equal to one hair on our legs! Do you think you can compensate us with money? You could back in those days. Now we are scared neither of you nor your money. You think you can solve things by buying us?'

'Seri! What do you want us to do? Spell it out!' the elder from their street said.

'Good! Transfer the two-acre field with the pump-set to this girl. And if something like this happens again your head will be severed from your body!'

'Yappa, how can that be? Can anyone let a two-acre

field go just for this? If you like, we will put in some more money. Let it go at that.'

'Register two acres now or else report to the court. We will discuss it there.'

When he heard this, Maruthappan intervened, 'I will transfer the land to her. My name will be mud if the case gets to court. My honour and prestige will be at stake.'

'These fellows are not like they were before. We better give them the land,' said Maruthappan's people and transferred the land.

'That's how it was back in those days, they were dumb creatures. Now, touch one of them and the whole lot will come swarming like a colony of bees. These are bad times!' So saying, they left, taking Maruthappan with them.

'Aamada, Velusami! It is only now that we have opened our eyes and can see things better. And they try to gouge out our eyes so that we can't see! That's how it was those days. Will they dare do that now? They may say they can, but they can't!' Thatha posed the question and answered it himself.

'Even my father was telling me, Thatha! In his time, he would sit on a chair in the courtyard of our house. When upper-caste people came by he would quickly get up, and it was only after they had passed by that he could sit down again. Otherwise they would abuse him, asking why Parayars needed a chair, and that too in the presence of their landlords!'

'That's true, that's how it was those days. Who cares now whether a landlord comes by or a mendicant! Our fellows will remain sitting, one leg thrown over the other. We didn't have these brains then!'

Masanam Thatha was not seen around for quite some time after this. When he came back to the village after a month, he was asked where he had been. In a village named Kattupatti, he said. He was a watchman in a sugarcane field. He went about his business quietly after he returned, and then suddenly, he caused a stir.

A couple of days earlier he had gone to water that Ashokar Ayya's cotton field. In the evening, after finishing the watering, it seems he went to Ashokar Ayya's house to collect his wages. Four or five landlords were sitting on a bench in the front verandah talking to Ashokar Ayya. When Thatha asked for his wages, Ayya gestured to him, asking him to wait. Thatha waited for about half an hour, then went and sat in the empty spot at one corner of the bench. At once, all those fellows jumped up in shock.

Ashokar Ayya's anger knew no limits. 'Enda, Parayar dog!' he shouted angrily. 'How dare you sit on the same bench as us? I am letting you off without harm only because you are an old man, otherwise I would have kicked you to death!'

Masanam Thatha shouted back, 'Dei, Ashokar! Don't jump around too much! You call me a Parayar dog, you pig-like fellow born to a sow? I waited for half an hour—you should have paid me and sent me off. I sat down because of the pain in my legs. What's wrong with that? We are all human beings! What do you think we are? Everyone jumping up when I sit down! If that's how much you respect me, well and good! Unlike in those days, see what happens now! People from your own caste get up with respect when I sit down. Just repeat what you said earlier and my slippers will give you my reply.'

Having said that, he returned to the street and merrily narrated this story again and again. Everyone who heard it said, 'He may belong to those days, but he still has spirit!' Thatha laughed, 'That's how it was, those days. Now we won't spare anyone, not even if he comes armed with two tusks. Aama!'

So saying, he pulled a beedi from behind his ear, lit it and took a long drag from it.

Ponnuthayi

Ponnuthayi must be around thirty or thirty-two; a robust woman. It's been seven or eight years since she got married, and in this time, she has given birth to four boys, one after the other. Ponnuthayi's skin is so dark that it is darker than night. She's also quite good-looking. Her children were darker than her. They lolled around in the street looking like baby crows. You could wipe each of them with your fingers, like their mother, and put a black bindi on your forehead.

Ponnuthayi had an excellent physique. When she walked the force of her gait shook the ground. Other women would talk disparagingly of her, asking whether this was any way a woman should walk! Same thing when she spoke. She had a bronze throat from which the words rang out loud and clear. When she stood at the street tap, her voice carried to the other end of the street. She always spoke to the point and hit the bull's eye. Most people did not like her one bit.

Many people in the village didn't know her as Ponnuthayi, only as Big Lips. Not just lips, they would say she was a Big Mouth. They resented the fact that she survived doing business, unlike the other women who worked as wage labourers for landlords.

Though Ponnuthayi was uneducated, she would board the bus to the town nearby, bring fruits and vegetables from there and make a living by selling them from house to house. No one else did that on her street. Unmindful of people's bad-mouthing, she stuck to her trade with determination.

One day Ponnuthayi brought a basketful of coconuts and went around the streets crying, 'Coconuts... coconuts... Three for ten rupees!'

One woman could not contain herself. 'If we buy coconuts from the plantation, we can get one for two rupees! Look at this woman doing her business so shamelessly!'

Right there she got into serious trouble.

'I never go looking for a fight, but if a fight comes my way, I never leave it. If you want to buy, buy, otherwise shut up! Who are you to talk about business?' retorted Ponnuthayi, and moved to the street farther down. But even after reaching there, instead of calling out 'Coconuts!' she started off with, 'I may go to work, or I may not. That's my business. Why should these people born of whores talk about me? Looks like they get heartburn if I do business! If anyone speaks about me with their tongues between their teeth, I will slice them off!'

Shaken by how she strode by, no one dared to ask her what she had in her basket. The women opened their mouths only when she was out of earshot.

'Look at her, walking away so arrogantly! Why can't

she toil like the rest of the village to earn her daily meal? She wants to do business like some upper-caste person! She's too much!' After Muniyamma said this, Ponnuthayi, who had gone to the west street, came back to the east side, and the conversation stopped immediately.

Ponnuthayi came up to the women and started shouting again, 'That day, when I was in my backyard brushing my teeth with toothpaste, some whore-borns were gaping and whispering among themselves. And why? I buy toothpaste and I brush my teeth with it! Why should they get heartburn because of that?'

After Ponnuthayi left, Akasampattikkari spoke up. 'Some Big Lips! Just look how she left! The kind of life she has, she can't even brush her teeth with her finger! What she drinks is koozh, but what she washes her bottom with is chilli rasam.'

Athiyamma responded, 'Don't say anything that will fall on her ears, mathini. If it does, she will shred you to pieces. Don't think she's not smart, she even had her own husband, who tied the knot with her, beaten up by the police!'

This police case is something that everyone talks about in the village. For the last two years, Ponnuthayi has been living alone after leaving her husband. She buys something to cook from the money that she makes from her business, and sleeps at her mother's place.

When she got married to Mookkandi she went with him in the hope that, like other women, she would also live happily. Though Mookkandi was thin, his moustache was really thick. He twirled his moustache all the time.

Twirling it day after day, both ends had become as sharp as horns, good to stab anyone. He went to work for four days and remained at home for three, but he never stopped eating at the local restaurants. In the evenings he would go and gobble up idlis, dosais, vadais and whatnot there, then return home at night and eat up the rice, too. If he didn't eat at the restaurants, he would feel he hadn't eaten at all. Whatever he earned, he spent on himself. The days he didn't go to work he fought with Ponnuthayi, trying to grab her wages so he could go out. If it was a Sunday, he had to buy meat for a curry and also drink the arrack that Mariappathevar brewed. Or else he would find something to fight with Ponnuthayi over and harass her.

Ponnuthayi ground her teeth and put up with all this. In the early days of her marriage, she somehow managed with her earnings. Later, with four children born one after the other, filling even one belly proved difficult. She tried hard to make both ends meet. She got a milch cow, looked after it, looked after her children, worked in the fields, worked at home and was completely exhausted at the end of all that. One day, Mookkandi upped and sold her cow but didn't give her any money for it. It was after the ensuing fight, having been beaten black and blue, that Ponnuthayi came back to her mother's place.

When she left her husband, her youngest child was still nursing. She brought only him with her. In four or five months, she weaned him. Then she left him at her husband's house and returned alone.

'What kind of woman is she? Not one bit of love for

her own children! Roaming around like a man! Have you ever seen a woman leave her children with her husband like this?'

Though tongues continued to wag in the village, Ponnuthayi was quite unconcerned. 'Are the children only mine? It was to ward off his violence that I gave birth to them, one by one. After two I wanted to stop, but he objected and brought me back. Now let him look after them himself,' said Ponnuthayi to herself.

Mookkandi was at his wits' end looking after the children. After putting up with it for quite long, he finally accosted Ponnuthayi one day and said, 'Ei, come home!'

'You and I have no relationship with each other now,' Ponnuthayi said. 'Whatever there was, finished two years back. I don't want to live with you anymore.' And she went on her way.

'What! A fool of a girl telling a man to his face that she doesn't want to live with him?' Mookkandi couldn't help shouting. 'You...are you a woman? Bitch who roams around like a whore without a care for her children!'

'I will do whatever I want to. Who are you to question me? Did I give birth to the children without your help? Try and bring them up,' Ponnuthayi shouted back angrily.

Mookkandi's rage knew no bounds. He yelled, 'Ei, you whore, shut your mouth. Look at your shape and your lips, if it was anyone else, he would never have married you if he saw your lips. I married you because I was an innocent. I should be beaten with slippers!'

'Not just slippers, with a broom, too. Useless fellow! But you will learn nothing even then.' She spat at him, but he caught her by the hair and slapped her four or five times. Then he dragged her away, beating her all the time.

Ponnuthayi tried to free herself by twisting her hands and legs, then grabbed his hand and bit it sharply. Wincing with pain, Mookkandi delivered a kick to Ponnuthayi's belly. Screaming with pain, Ponnuthayi landed on a wooden pounder lying nearby and split her head. Blood streamed out. Her clothes were soaked in it. She didn't scream or yell after that, she didn't even abuse him. The blood still spurting out, she ran towards the south, away from him.

'Ei, go and grab her! She is running towards the fields, she'll jump into some well and take her life for sure!' cried someone in the crowd.

'Let the whore get lost! I will bury that donkey and marry another woman. Are there no other women in this world?' declared Mookkandi unabashedly.

Ponnuthayi's mother ran after her with dishevelled hair. By this time, the entire village was in a commotion. Men and women, without exception, were in hot pursuit of Ponnuthayi.

But Ponnuthayi didn't go and jump into any well. Taking a short cut, she ran across the fields to the police station in the next village.

A huge crowd gathered in front of the station at the sight of Ponnuthayi, blood dripping from her head. The policemen took her inside and questioned her.

'Sir, my husband is always torturing me. I left him to live on my own two years ago. Today he came and harassed me again, beat me and split my head. Only you can do something now.' There was blood all over. After noting down her name, village, street, etc., a policeman asked her to go to the government hospital. By then, her mother had also reached and Ponnuthayi went there with her.

Don't know by whose grace, but that policeman turned out to be someone with sisters! He immediately sent two others to catch Mookkandi and bring him to the police station. By this time Ponnuthayi had also returned with her head bandaged.

Mookkandi was taken inside and beaten thoroughly. After putting him in the lock-up, the policeman asked Ponnuthayi, 'What do you say? We can keep your husband here for two days, put some sense into him and send him back. Will you agree to live with him? If he creates a problem again, just come and tell us.'

'Sir, do whatever you want with him, but I can't live with him now. I've suffered enough, I prefer to stay alone and survive somehow.' So saying, she guided her mother out and went home.

Mookkandi was let off the next day with a stern warning. By this time the entire village knew how Ponnuthayi had her husband beaten up at the police station. There was all kinds of loose talk about her.

'Whatever it is, can anyone report a man who tied the knot with her and get him beaten up at the police station? Isn't she an arrogant whore?' asked Athiyamma.

'Chi...don't talk like that. How long could she bear everything? Didn't she take all the beating he gave her? This kind of fellow should be handed over to the police. Only then will others stop being abusive,' said Kuruvamma.

'Oh-ho, going by what you're saying, sounds like the wife should hit the husband back if he beats her! Good idea! But how long do you think these policemen will protect her? We can't trust them! Wherever she goes, ultimately she has to come back to her husband, remember that! And won't he root out her arrogance then?' asked Athiyamma.

Kaniyamma, who was listening to all this, said, 'She left him two years back and has been living alone since then. He should have left it at that. He tried to take her back, she said no. It's he who created the problem. If you don't like something, you should just leave it and carry on.'

'Did he want her back so that he could live with her? No. He had a tough time managing four children, that's why he thought he would drag her back.'

When Kuruvamma said this, Kaniyamma intervened immediately, 'How long can he stay alone? Women can, but can men?'

While the women were discussing all this, the men too, were going back and forth. 'Is he a man? What a fool! She took him to the police station and got him beaten up, and he still lets her live! Useless fellow! I would have strangled her at the police station itself,' said Kuppusamy angrily.

'You're a real hero! No big thing, killing one's wife. He should have given her a beating or two from the very beginning to keep her under his thumb. Didn't do that, now he's suffering. If a man can't keep his wife under his control, he isn't a man! His moustache is an insult to him!' said Govindan, and laughed loudly.

When the men mocked him like this, Mookkandi's anger grew and grew. He ground his teeth and roamed south to north, north to south, wondering what to do. Then, having decided something, he went to Ponnuthayi's house. Calling her father out, he said, 'I am never going to take back your daughter and live with her. Let her bring her children here and bring them up. I will marry someone else, and go my way. I have been shamed too much by her.'

Ponnuthayi's father replied calmly, 'Please be patient, mappilai. They say a woman's wisdom is late in realizing things. That day the foolish girl went to the station through ignorance. Give me a few more days, I myself will advise her well and bring her over.'

'That won't do. I don't want her any more. I will leave the children here. That's all.' And Mookkandi turned to leave.

Ponnuthayi, who was listening to all this silently, said, 'Why leave the children here? They are your children, you take care of them. I want neither you nor the children I got from you! Is there a law that only the mother should look after the children? Don't bring them here, and don't you dare show your face here again. Be warned!'

Mookkandi left in a great rage. Ponnuthayi's mother wailed loudly and said, 'He is going to get some other woman and live with her. She will harass your children.

Listen to me! Made of stone or made of grass, for a woman her husband is everything. Instead of lying at his feet, you are here. Pathakathi! At least take the children and bring them up here.'

'Stop crying and keep quiet for a while, Amma. Don't fathers know how to bring up their children? Let them try. It's enough that we have lived by marrying stones and grass.' So saying, Ponnuthayi went inside the house and came back with a blade in her hands. She sat on top of the chicken coop in front of the house, and taking the blade, slashed the wedding-knot around her neck and removed the thali.

Seeing this, her mother screamed, 'You mad whore, what have you done? Eduvatta peyamagale! What has happened is not normal! Which woman will slash the knot that a man has tied around her neck? I should have given birth to a stone pestle instead of you!' And picking up the knot from the ground she wept bitterly.

Hearing her crying so loudly, four or five people came to the house and began abusing Ponnuthayi. She didn't bother. Instead, she took on her mother, 'Amma, will you stop your wailing? Do you want the whole village to know what has happened? I'm going to town. You go to the kamma-bank and pluck some kozha to feed the lamb. Innocent, dumb creature, it's so hungry.'

Ponnuthayi put the thali in her waist-fold, picked up her basket and went to town. The next day she put up a small shop in front of the chavady and started her business. The thali that had lain around her neck for ten years occupied the entire shop now, in the form of goods to be sold.

Half-sari

'I told him again and again, don't send our daughter so far away. Did he listen? No. Now we are the most miserable creatures alive, unable even to look at the face of the dear child we gave birth to!' Arulayi wailed loudly as she kept up this refrain.

The women, watching her beat her head and bosom as she wailed, tried hard to console her, but Arulayi was inconsolable. Outside the house, her husband Irulappan sat on the verandah, totally shattered.

All the people gathered there stood around as if they had seen a ghost, confused about what to say or do next.

'Not for nothing did they say that money has power even over the nether world. The fellow has cash, he can suppress everything.'

When Irulappan's father said this, Kaliappan, Arulayi's brother, shouted angrily, 'So, he can hide a whole pumpkin in a heap of rice and we have to just sit around and watch!'

Kaliappan was around twenty or twenty-five years old. From the moment he heard that his sister's daughter, Chellakkili, had died suddenly he had gone quite mad, muttering constantly about this and that. He took his brother-in-law, Irulappan, with him and set off immediately for Kuppampattanam that very night. Though they lost no time going, they were forced to return without being able to see Chellakkili's dead body.

Chellakkili was eleven years old, but her body was already in full bloom. Of the seven children born to Arulayi, the first four had died and of the other three, Chellakkili was the youngest. Irulappan and Arulayi worked on Jegannatha Naicker's farmland. Their first two sons did not study beyond the third standard. They looked after the two buffaloes in the house, plucking grass to feed them, and grazing them, and sometimes doing some wage-labour.

Irulappan had a great desire that their daughter Chellakkili should somehow study up to the eighth standard at least. And so he brought himself to send her far away to school.

When Chellakkili was in the fifth standard, his landlord asked him, 'Elay! Irulappa! What is your daughter doing now?'

'She is studying in the fifth, sami. That's why I am struggling so hard. She must finish her eighth, even if I have to borrow money for that,' replied Irulappan.

'Poda, mad fellow! What's the use of studying up to the eighth standard these days? How many boys are there loitering around without a job after studying this and that! Only if she studies up to the twelfth can she even try for the job of a teacher,' said the landlord.

Irulappan, who was watering the landlord's chilli

plants, straightened up. Leaning on the handle of his spade, he looked at the landlord in surprise. 'It is my wish to give her a very high education, sami! But I don't have the means, and our local school only goes up to the eighth standard.'

'My daughter lives in Kuppampattanam. She has sent a letter saying she needs a young girl to help her with the housework. If you say yes, I will take your daughter to her. She can live and eat there and do whatever work there is. There is a big school there, let her study there. She can do some work before going to school and the rest after coming back. She can help my daughter. She will pay Chellakkili some amount of money every month. What do you say?' he asked, and waited for a response.

'Even if we could send her for the sake of her studies, her mother will not leave her, Sami. She will not part with her Chellakkili,' said Irulappan.

'What are you saying, le? Whenever you feel like seeing your daughter, just tell me, I will spend my own money to take you both to meet her.'

When the landlord said this, Irulappan's ambition for his daughter grew. He felt a real thrill, imagining Chellakkili studying to become a teacher.

'Anyway, I will discuss this with Arulayi and then tell you, sami,' Irulappan replied and resumed his watering. As he looked at each chilli plant with its white flowers and red fruit, Chellakkili filled his mind with dreams of her living happily, like these plants in full bloom.

As soon as he reached home that evening, he called out to Arulayi and repeated whatever the landlord had told him, in the hope that she would agree with his suggestion. He looked at her expectantly, waiting for her response.

'Would you ask me this if you had the least bit of love for your child? We have only one daughter and we have brought her up like the apple of our eyes. How can we send her somewhere out of sight and still live? We don't want that kind of education for her. Let her study as much she can in our village, that's all!'

But Irulappan did not leave it at that. He continued the discussion while he ate.

'I am bringing up Chellakkili without allowing her even to move one small thing from here to there. We don't have to make our innocent baby do household work somewhere else in order to get by! Let her remain with us, drinking koozh or plain water!' After Arulayi's outburst, Irulappan fell silent for some time.

Later, chewing on the betel leaves in his mouth, he said, 'Etha! Just think about it for a moment. Is she going to be doing hard labour to survive? No. She will go to school, tha, and help with the housework when she is free. Moreover, our landlord himself is taking her there, he will arrange for everything.'

However hard Irulappan tried to convince her, Arulayi would not budge. Because of this they both had heated arguments every day. Finally, when it was confirmed that the landlord would bring Chellakkili back as soon as the examinations were over and vacations had begun, Arulayi consented, half-heartedly.

After she passed fifth standard and was about to enter

the sixth, Irulappan got a transfer certificate from the school and gave it to the landlord. Because it was the first time she was going away, Irulappan tried hard to persuade the landlord to let him accompany his daughter. But the landlord dissuaded him, saying he had harvesting and paddy transplanting work to do, so he took Chellakkili alone with him to Kuppampattanam.

It was now eight months since Chellakkili had started work. In all this time she was not taken back to her village even once. When the landlord was asked, he replied gruffly, 'Will your daughter vanish? I went and saw her only last month. She has put on weight with all the good food she's getting. Hardly any work to do. You yourself will not recognize your daughter if you see her now.' So saying, he went on his way.

'I am thinking of at least sending her a letter, mothalali, please give me the address.' Irulappan took the address to a literate fellow in his own street and sent his daughter a letter. He waited and waited, hoping she would reply, but he waited in vain.

Arulayi kept pestering him, telling him to go and see his daughter. She scraped together some money by cutting expenses here and there. 'Take Kaliappan along without telling the landlord, look for this address and go and meet our child,' she said, giving her husband the money she had saved. She also gave them some roasted rice and groundnuts for Chellakkili.

Just as Irulappan was getting ready to leave, came the news that Chellakkili had died all of a sudden. For the first time the landlord came to their street that day and went to Irulappan's house to explain things clearly.

'Start immediately. Let us at least see her face,' he said sorrowfully.

The moment he heard the news the world went dark before Irulappan's eyes. He did not know how to contain himself and go home to tell his wife.

It was Kaliappan who roused him from his grieving state and convinced him to accompany him to Kuppampattanam. As soon as they reached there Kaliappan realized what had happened.

A huge crowd had gathered in front of the landlord's daughter's house. When her father introduced Irulappan and Kaliappan, she wiped her face with the end of her sari, as if she was crying.

Neither Irulappan nor Kaliappan could say a word. Bursting with sorrow all they could do was to sit and stare at her vacantly. The landlord's daughter said, 'This time yesterday, the poor thing was alive. Did I know that she would die suddenly like this? The child who was sitting studying suddenly started throwing her hands and legs this way and that and fell down in a fit. Frothing at the mouth. I was so shocked I couldn't move. We got a taxi and she was taken immediately to the hospital in town and given four-five bottles of glucose. One injection cost four hundred rupees, but I didn't care about the money. She was given two injections, but even after all that her life couldn't be saved. What else could I do?' she said and wiped the tears from her eyes.

'The doctor asked us to cremate her immediately. I pleaded with him to wait for her parents, but he insisted that the body should not be kept there for long. If you had told me that she was suffering from such an illness, I would not have allowed her to work here at all. You left her here, keeping all this from me, and she had to go and die in my house! Appa!' Before his daughter could finish, the landlord went to her and hugged her tightly.

Four or five people who were living as tenants in the daughter's house, came up and said, 'Seri, what has happened has happened. Whether she was in her village or here, if she was fated to die, who could stop it? Do whatever you can now, and then see them off with kindness.' By speaking like this they made everything look normal.

The landlord gave Irulappan a thousand rupees and said, 'What can one say? Do those who have departed ever come back, even if we cry year after year? Be brave. Here, take this and return to the village. I myself will come back after two days.' Irulappan and Kaliappan did not open their mouths, did not so much as glance at the money, but went to the bus-stand to catch the bus back to their village.

But as soon as they reached, they overheard four or five people discussing Chellakkili's death. Their blood froze.

'Even if they are so rich, is this the way to bring someone home to work and then murder her? It's all that widow's handiwork—she has done it so carefully that everything remains hidden.'

'So what if she has lost her man? Do you know how many fellows she has under her thumb who will support her?'

'I saw that child washing clothes in the morning, but by three in the afternoon that dreadful woman had killed her.'

'Which village is she from? How did that whore-widow kill her?'

'She was brought here on the pretext that she could study, but she was not sent to school at all. She was made to work non-stop. That ten- or twelve-year-old child had to do all the household work, cleaning, cooking and whatnot! The smallest mistake, her two sons would pull up her skirt and spank her bottom. This my wife told me.'

'Often her sons and their friends would misbehave with that child. This the mother also knew, but she ignored everything. She wouldn't let that child step out of the house.'

'Did they poison her or give her some drugs?'

'No, no! She ordered her to prepare the rice-batter by three and went into town. It was past four when the child finished. Seems she was hit on her neck with a log of wood. One blow which landed in the wrong place. The child was lying there, writhing and thrashing about. When she started frothing at the mouth they got scared and took her to the doctor, but she died on the way. That's why they came back and burnt the body immediately. Her father and uncle had come, but they could not even see the dead body. They have paid money to those in the know and settled everything. Her father is an innocent fellow, a dumb creature. Went away without a word.'

Kaliappan was unable to bear it any longer. Exploding with anger and frustration he dragged his brother-in-law along and reached their village, but told him not to say anything to Arulayi.

When the landlord returned, Kaliappan took Irulappan to his house. When he saw the landlord, it was sorrow more than rage that overcame Irulappan. He could not utter a word. It was Kaliappan who started shouting heatedly, but surprisingly, the landlord took both of them inside the house and tried consoling them with a show of love and sympathy.

Kaliappan realized exactly what the landlord was doing. 'Don't try to fool us with all this pretence. I know everything, about all the cruelties you inflicted on the child, I know that you killed her. Don't show me your chameleon character,' he yelled.

'Look here, Kaliappa! Don't lie so blatantly, saying that she was killed. Etho, it was her fate, she departed! Here, take this, there are two thousand rupees in it.'

But this only made Kaliappan more furious. 'What do you mean? Are you placing a value of two thousand rupees on Chellakkili's life?' He lunged forward to hit the landlord.

The landlord responded calmly, 'Kaliappa, don't behave rashly in anger. Do you know how lovingly my daughter looked after Chellakkili? She even told me that Chellakkili should be given a thavani to wear. She was planning to bring her here during the vacation, wearing the half-sari. But all this happened before she could do so. Look here, if you don't believe me, here is the half-sari my daughter bought for her to wear. She packed it along with Chellakkili's other clothes and gave it to me, saying it would remind her of Chellakkili.' Then he showed Kaliappan a red thavani.

Kaliappan's fury knew no bounds. 'You said you would send the child to school, but you sent her to the cremation ground instead! And you still have the nerve to speak! We know what happened there. You and your thavani!' Kaliappan flung the cloth aside angrily and stormed off. Irulappan stood there for a moment looking down at the red thavani. Then, as if something had crossed his mind, he suddenly bent, picked it up and hurried home.

The next morning, a dead body was seen hanging from a red thavani on the neem tree in the backyard of the landlord's house.

Freedom

Their house was as big as a bungalow. Only Ayya and Amma lived in that huge place. Both were easily more than seventy, Ayya might even have been past eighty. Though they had four sons, none of them lived with their parents. They all worked in places far away, where they lived with their wives and children. If they felt like it, they would visit once in a blue moon.

Ayya and Amma had many servants to look after their needs, but the main one was Arayi. With her was a twelve-year-old boy, Subramani, who did odd jobs for Ayya. There were also a dog and a cat in the house. The dog's name was Nikki. The cat would come running if you called her Pussy. Subramani took care of the dog and cat, bathing them, feeding them, leashing and unleashing them, cleaning up their shit and all that. Nikki and he would play like friends.

There was a small hut at the back of the bungalow where Arayi and Subramani stayed. Apart from them, there was Saraswati, who did the cooking. To shop for milk and medicines, to go to the post office, bank or any such chores, there was a man named Chinnasami. The driver was Murugan. For gardening, an old man named Kuppusami. So many servants. All of them came in the morning and left by the evening. At noon everyone would be served their meals. Only Arayi and Subramani stayed inside the house and worked. They were not from the same village. Arayi cooked the meals for all the other servants, and for the dog and the cat, with rice bought from the ration shop.

Arayi's parents had died before she was ten years old, she was their eldest daughter. She became a servant girl at the age of ten. She worked in some household or other and also looked after her younger brothers and sisters. She had worked in many different places for forty years before coming to this place. She was more than fifty now. She had never had the chance to get married and now there was no one to get her married to. Here, in Ayya's house, apart from food, she was paid a hundred rupees per month. Though the younger brothers and sisters she had taken care of were all well off now, none of those wretches cared two hoots about her. Even at this age, Arayi was forced to work hard every day. If she ever rested for some time, Amma would get angry.

Arayi would rise early, sprinkle water at the doorstep, sweep the front of the house, draw the kolam, water the potted plants all around the house, collect water at the tap, fill the cisterns, wash the clothes, clean the vessels and would always be busy with some work or the other in between. Around eight in the morning, Arayi and Subramani would get some coffee. Milk was bought by the litre in that house, but these two always only got black coffee. Around ten, both would be given some leftover kanji and pickle. Exactly at eleven, Arayi would light the fire in the hearth to cook rice for the other servants. After it was ready, she would make a curry with the stale vegetables that Amma gave her. She distributed the food only after measuring everything out properly. When the cooking was done, she would hand the meal for the dog and cat to Subramani. He'd go straight to Amma with the plates, who would put tiny pieces of bone in each one. He would mash the rice properly, supervised by Amma, and then call out to Nikki and Pussy and feed them. Amma would wait till both had eaten half the food and then leave.

As soon as they were finished, Subramani washed both plates, left them to dry in the sun and went over to Ayya. If he had no other work, he was supposed to wait on Ayya in his room.

Around one in the afternoon, Arayi would call Subramani to serve him his meal, only after which she'd eat. Before that she would have served all those who came to work from outside. Subramani was ten or twelve years old. As a growing boy, he would eat to his heart's content. Arayi fed him well even if it meant that she herself went hungry. When lunch was over, she would again wash the vessels and utensils. Around two, she would sit down to grind rice and black gram for the batter. She would first grind the rice and then the pulses for at least an hour. By the time she scooped out the batter from the grinder it would be four o'clock— if she finished before that Amma would get angry. Ayya and Amma did not like batter made in the electric grinder. Amma was satisfied only if Arayi ground the rice and gram in the stone grinder for at least two hours.

From dawn to dusk, Arayi and Subramani had to do some work or the other, but Amma was never satisfied, no matter how hard they worked. They thought Ayya was better in this respect. From the time Amma woke up in the morning till the minute she went to bed at night, her voice rang out continuously in the house: 'Arayi!' 'Subramani!' She kept finding fault with this and that. Sometimes she would suddenly catch hold of Subramani and rain blows on him. If he cried out, two more would land on him, with the admonition that he should not cry out so loudly. Unable to stand the pain, however, he couldn't help screaming. Whenever he got a beating, Subramani would run weeping to the mango tree on the south side of the house where Nikki would be tied up. Seeing him weep, the dog would give him a sympathetic look and wag his tail. Very soon, Subramani and the dog would be asleep together under the mango tree. And as soon as he woke up, he would receive a good scolding.

The servants were not allowed to speak to each other. In fact, they were forbidden to talk to anyone who lived in the neighbourhood. These were Ayya and Amma's strict orders. Sometimes Amma would take Ayya to the hospital in the car. That was one occasion when Arayi and Subramani could talk to each other freely. They would even talk to the neighbours, careful that no one noticed. At such times they would cry so bitterly that it was pathetic.

One day Ayya and Amma left in the car at daybreak itself for a blood test. Ayya had diabetes and his eyes were weak. He was also hard of hearing. Subramani, with a song on his lips, climbed the mango tree early in the morning and ate a mango in happy abandon. Arayi, too, sat near the well laughing and talking.

Chinnarani Teacher from the other side of the fence asked, 'No one at home? I can hear singing!'

'They have gone to the doctor, will return only after sunset. They will eat lunch at their daughter's house,' said Arayi.

'It's freedom day for me today, Teacher,' said Subramani, 'and freedom for this Paatti too.' And he plucked two mangoes and lobbed them to the teacher.

Then he scrambled down and unleashed the dog. 'Nikki, it's freedom for you, too, today! Run around till the evening, but see that you don't go outside. If you get lost, I'll lose my life.' Happy to be set free, Nikki began bounding around, circling Subramani. She also made four quick rounds of Arayi Paatti. Then she peed on the mango tree, and didn't stop running for a single moment.

Subramani unbuttoned his shorts and peed on the curry-leaf plant. While peeing he said, 'Paatti, Amma plucks leaves from this plant for cooking. Let her do that now!'

'Elay, you are becoming more brash by the day. Why do all this just because you are angry with Amma? The plant will wither if you pee on it,' said Arayi.

'It won't wither, Paatti, it will grow faster! She makes me suffer so much, let her cook with my pee now and eat,' said Subramani grandly.

Arayi thought how much anger and pain there must be in the little boy's heart and said, 'If Amma saw that you had peed on the plant, she would grab your thing and cut it off. Remember that!' Though she scolded him, Arayi was also filled with a wicked kind of happiness.

But Subramani didn't stop at that. He kicked the water cistern that Arayi had filled, sending the water splashing in all directions. Seeing this, Arayi exclaimed, 'Elay! I just filled the water to the brim. You've gone and dirtied it and spilled half. Amma will not spare you when she returns. Get up, you!' and she began chasing him but there was no anger on her face, only happiness.

Amma and Ayya came back in the evening. Arayi and Subramani pasted the grave look back on their faces and silently got back to their chores. After inspecting all the work that she had assigned them, Amma called out to the cat and dog, looked them over, and enquired of Subramani whether they had eaten. Good thing that Subramani had tied the dog up again before Amma came back.

The next morning Amma called out to Chinnarani Teacher and asked, 'Those lazy fellows working in my house, what were they doing in my absence yesterday? Did they tell you anything?'

'Nothing, Amma. I was also busy with housework, I didn't see them,' replied the teacher cautiously.

When Amma went for her bath, Arayi said quietly, 'Teacher, if Amma asks you, please tell her we didn't speak to you about anything. Look at me, I'm unmarried, no man's hand has touched my body, there aren't even worms growing in my belly, it still looks so young. But I'm getting older, Teacher, can I keep working and working like a young girl all the time? This Amma doesn't let me rest for a single second, doesn't let me go out anywhere. That poor boy, she harasses him so much. He's of school-going age, but the poor fellow had to land up here and suffer.'

Even as Arayi was speaking, Amma called out from the bathroom, 'Arayi, where are you? I can't find you.'

'I'm here, Amma, I'm putting the firewood out in the sun to dry.' Like a six-year-old girl, Arayi ran to where the firewood was stacked.

The teacher was filled with sympathy. 'Poor thing, even at this age she runs scared, toiling so hard just to fill her stomach!' Thinking such thoughts, the teacher went back inside.

A week later, Subramani was heard crying loudly early in the morning. Normally, he cried only when he was beaten, but it wasn't clear why he got a beating this time. In the afternoon, after Amma had gone for her nap, Subramani went up to the fence and called out to the teacher.

'Teacher,' he said mournfully, 'why don't you take me away from here somehow? Please put me into your school. In my village I studied up to the fourth. I really want to study, Teacher. I haven't eaten anything since the morning today. I broke the phenyl bottle by mistake, Teacher. She beat me for that and said I wouldn't get any food. Paatti somehow gave me a little rice secretly, but Amma found out and scolded her, too. Please get me admitted into a school, Teacher, at least I will get a meal at noon.' Subramani began weeping bitterly.

The teacher didn't know what to say. She brought two bananas and gave them to him. 'Eat these quickly and go back. If Amma finds out, she will scold me, too.' Subramani hid behind the wall of the well, ate the bananas, then drank some water.

When Arayi came by to dispose of the garbage, Subramani said happily, 'Paatti, I'm going to join a school and study. I have told the Teacher, she will get me admitted. You want to come, Paatti? I won't go away and leave you here. You speak to the Teacher, too, Paatti.'

After the exams were over and vacations began, the teacher went away to her mother's house. Subramani didn't like living in Amma's house at all, he was always unhappy and depressed. For that too, he got a scolding from Amma.

One day she caught hold of him and started abusing him roundly. 'You dumb fool, is there some treasure buried here for you? Did your father and mother come and dump it here? What if your mother only gets fifty rupees for the kind of work you do, don't you eat your fill like a dog? Your body starts aching only when you have to work! The rascal doesn't even wash his bum after shitting! This is what happens when you pick up a beggar from the street and bring him home! Bend down and he farts, straighten up and he stretches his arms over his head, cracking knuckles! What sort of work can I get out of the fellow! Can't find anyone else either, otherwise I would have driven this donkey away with a broomstick.'

Arayi and Subramani listened to her without moving and, this time, Subramani did not cry. But Arayi wiped away a tear that slowly welled up in her eyes. Subramani looked at her miserably. Amma started shouting again. 'Why are you standing there, Arayi? Why are you blowing your nose? Feel bad when he's scolded? Go and start pounding the soaked rice. My daughter is coming, I have to make athirasam for her to take away.'

Arayi walked away slowly. Subramani followed. Amma started shouting again, 'You! Why are you following her around like her tail? Bring the spade and clear the grass here. Everything should be spick and span when my daughter comes. Now get going!'

Subramani fetched the spade but was weeping as he bent down and began clearing the grass. Arayi, too, wept as she pounded the rice. After they finished their work, Amma called them to give them some coffee, but as soon as she was out of sight both of them threw the coffee away.

The next morning Amma called out, 'Arayi... Subramani!' as usual, but there was no one there to do her bidding.

Old Man and a Buffalo

Just meeting Malandi Thatha and talking to him, all our sorrows would vanish as if by magic. His face shone with happiness all the time. No one ever saw him deep in sorrow. Even when he was in bed with a broken leg, he was his usual cheerful self. He always spoke with laughter in his voice, and was the same with kids as he was with old men. Everyone enjoyed talking to him.

Thatha was neither very tall nor very short. He always wore a white veshti around his waist with a bulge in the waistfold, as if a packet was tucked inside it. It held some betel leaves, areca nuts, a lime-box, snuff-box, tobacco-box, etc. And some rupee notes and coins. When children asked him for money, he would pick out a five- or ten-paisa coin from there and give it to them. If they were eating something when Thatha passed by, they would share a small portion with him. Thatha would gladly partake of it. He had a white towel slung over his shoulder, and sometimes he would act like he was going to beat the kids with it and the kids in turn would pretend to be scared and run from him, laughing.

Thatha's face always glowed, and he was always

shaved by the barber who sat under the neem tree at the end of the street. Whenever he was there, Thatha regaled the young crowd standing around with his jokes. They didn't lag behind either, matching him joke for joke.

Malandi Thatha's wife had died long back, leaving behind no children. Though he hadn't been too old then, he didn't remarry. His relatives tried many times to convince him to marry again, but Thatha didn't relent. Didn't he need a woman to at least cook some kanji for him, they wondered aloud, but he countered by asking whether he didn't have two hands to boil up some kanji for himself.

Back in the day there used to be only two people who grazed all the village cattle in Kuppayapatti—one was Irulandi and the other, Veeran. Irulandi used to graze buffaloes, Veeran grazed calves and cows. The village cattle would be taken to the banks of the kamma or to the fields and left there to graze. In the evening they would be herded back. Irulandi and Veeran were paid one rupee per animal, per month. Every morning, even as dawn was just breaking, the two men would go from house to house, untie the cattle and herd them together. In the evening they were brought back and let loose in the village. The cattle would find their way back to their pens by themselves. On an average, Veeran and Irulandi made about two hundred rupees a month. For Pongal or Deepavali they would get five or ten rupees extra. Sometimes the upper-caste farmers would also gift them a veshti or two.

Irulandi used to take his son along when he went out

grazing. If the cattle strayed too far, he would send his son to herd them back. Malandi was his son, and he was very happy being with his father on such occasions. He started grazing cattle from those days and had not done any other job since. It was said that Malandi was very lively even as a child. His greatest joy was to take a ride on top of the buffaloes. If the cattle were grazing near the pond, he would pluck the cucumbers or maize growing there and eat them on the sly, or he'd catch fish from the pond to roast. He passed the time like that.

After Irulandi died, Malandi continued grazing the village cattle for some time, but when that did not work out well for him, he began rearing a buffalo calf himself. He took that she-buffalo out alone to graze. His father used to be called Village Grazer Irulandi, and even after Malandi stopped doing that job, the name stuck to him too. If you said Village Grazer Malandi everyone knew who that was, even though there were two or three other Malandis in the village.

Malandi must have been around fifty. He survived on just one buffalo. Whenever a calf was born, he would sell the mother and keep the calf. In the mornings he would take the buffalo to the fields. He would sit on the bund and chew some betel leaves while it grazed. Later he would spread a towel out on the bund to relax for some time. When the sun got too strong, he would tie the towel around his head. With a stick in his hands he would keep calling out to the buffalo, producing several sounds like...eiii, deiiii, elay, mmmm, tha. Around two in the afternoon he would wash the buffalo down and herd her back home. But while bathing her he would keep talking to her. The boys who were grazing cattle with him would laugh at this and crack jokes together.

One day Malandi was bathing his buffalo in the pond. As usual, he was talking to her. Nearby, the others were also bathing the cattle they were in charge of.

'Elay! Be still! You have mud all over your body. See those curved horns? Look how clean they are now. This is because I look after you so well. Don't I wash you down every day, scrubbing away all the dirt?' He splashed some more water on the buffalo, but when he began scrubbing her, she stepped out of the water. 'Dei, keep still! Don't run away. Just look at your mug! Where did you go and stick it to have got so much muck on it? I knew it when you went grazing with that Palaniappan's cow! Didn't I tell you not to befriend her? She's a very mischievous cow. You must have had a good roll in the slime in the field...' So saying, he started scrubbing her head vigorously. While this was going on the buffalo lifted her tail.

'Now...why lift your tail? How come you always feel like peeing or shitting only when you bathe? Okay, okay, go ahead, but it is useful only if you drop it on the ground, not in the water!' He said, holding her nose-cord firmly. When she finished, he splashed some water on her behind.

Kandasami, who was bathing his cow nearby, said, 'Thatha, you keep talking to your buffalo every day, does she understand anything?'

'Elay! Do you think she listens to me without

understanding? Look! When I wash her, she turns whichever way I ask her to. Don't you see that?'

'I didn't, Thatha, I didn't see the buffalo turn. It is only you who's circling around and splashing water and scrubbing!'

But Thatha just laughed and changed the subject.

'Elay! Have you ever gone to the sugarcane field of that Guava Fruit Naicker and grazed your cattle there? There's a big monitor lizard in that field, I have seen it many times. Somehow or the other I'm going to catch it one day. When I saw it yesterday the stupid creature ran like mad. Off I went chasing it, when it fell into the canal with a big splash and swam away like a crocodile. I blew it completely! I should have caught it the moment it started swimming! Its head was above the water and it was looking in all directions while it swam, just like a snake!'

'What will you do with the monitor lizard if you catch it, Thatha?'

'Listen to the fool! What will I do with it?! It does wonders for the body if one makes a curry with it, it's like medicine. You know, you can't get monitor lizard curry that easily!'

'You're quite something, Thatha! Let me spy it. One shot from the sling is all I need! It will die twitching!' boasted Kandasami.

'Okay, you go to the sugarcane field one day and get that monitor lizard—we'll see then!' So saying, Thatha left for home.

Another day Kandasami's sister, Maruthayi, came

to graze the cattle. She was seven or eight years old, born four or five years after Kandasami. Malandi Thatha accosted her with a laugh and asked, 'Ei, you thieving kid! What made you come this way today? Not married yet? Want to marry me? I will feed you rice and curry every day.'

'Go and ask your own granddaughter! Don't you say such things to my sister!' Maruthayi's brother spoke up for her.

'Do I have only one granddaughter? Aren't all the girls in the village my granddaughters?'

'So Thatha, why did you never get married? Isn't it because you don't have a wife that they sing songs about you?' Kandasami asked.

'They sing that song about *me*? Your grandmother died after I got married. I used to roam around singing that song when I was your age, grazing the cattle.'

You, village grazer!
A leg with a sore!
No wife to care for you
Scratch, scratch that sore!

'What's the time now, Thatha?' Kandasami asked.

'Can't you tell from the light? It's time to milk the cattle. Take yours home. Escort this dark-skinned girl back as well. I'll come next week for the engagement!' And he pinched Maruthayi's cheek playfully. Slapping his hand, Maruthayi caught hold of her calf and dragged it away.

Not a single man washed his cattle at the kamma that day. Since it looked like it might rain, they let the cattle into the water and left. Malandi Thatha was the only one washing his buffalo. He kept talking to her even as he scrubbed her down.

'Elay! I've been seeing this every day. When you graze, some ten or twenty white storks hover around you...why is that? Are they your partners? Wherever you go, all the storks follow you as if in a procession. Very funny, da! Intha, why whip me with your tail? Swish it at the mosquitoes if they're biting you, why use it on me, you rascal?' he said, bending down and scrubbing the dirt off her legs. 'Aammale, why walk around with that black sparrow on your back all the time? And I can't help laughing when you walk around like that, the white storks around you, swaying your body lazily. Even that Kandasami fellow told me the other day that the white storks and black sparrows are your friends. Is that true, le?'

While Malandi was jabbering away, Eenjediyan came walking along the kamma-bank. He was the same age as Malandi. 'What's the matter, Malandi,' he said, 'Talking to yourself? Have you gone nuts like that blind fellow?'

'Oh, is it you, Eenjediyan? What did you say, talking to myself? Look, I was talking to this moodhevi! She never answers back, not even once. Seri. Why are you here at this time of day? The sky has turned dark, it may rain.' So saying, he goaded his buffalo out of the water.

'I came out to shit and thought I would wash my feet here. Then I heard your voice and found you here, speaking all by yourself. Seri, I'm going home. Bring your buffalo along, we'll walk together.'

Letting the buffalo lead them, they both followed, talking to each other. Malandi loosened the veshti he had worn like a loin-cloth, untied the towel he'd worn like a turban and wiped his face with it.

'She's pregnant, looks like she will deliver in two or three months!' Eenjediyan commented.

'Yes, she's pregnant, that's why I'm taking good care of her. After she delivers, I will pay all my debts and sit back.'

'You are single, what kind of debts do you have? You don't have children.'

'You're right! But last year, didn't I slip from the bund while grazing my buffalo and break my leg? You remember? I had to borrow two hundred rupees from that Rajaram Ayya for the treatment. I have been paying back only the interest, the loan still remains. On interest itself I have paid back more than a thousand rupees. Now, when the buffalo delivers, he will catch hold of her and take her away against the loan. Only the calf will remain with me.'

'You'll let the buffalo go for a two-hundred-rupee loan?'

'Have I let her go yet? That's what he says! Let her deliver, then we'll see.' So saying, he drove the buffalo home.

The next day, while grazing cattle in the fields that Kandasami fellow was joined by four or five more boys; Madan, Masilamani, Murukesan and two others. Spying a snake that slithered towards the canal Mani yelled, 'Ealaika! A snake! Ei! Look, look at it rushing that way! Unkappanoli! There it is, hiding in the grass!'

Old Man and a Buffalo

Hearing the commotion, Malandi Thatha left his buffalo in the adjoining field and came over. 'Ei! Cowards! Screaming so loudly at the sight of a water-snake? I came running, thinking something was wrong! Make way, let me take a look. I will crush his arrogance now.' Saying this, he took the stick used for grazing, pressed the snake to the ground with it and caught its head with his bare hands. Then he made his way to the fig tree. All the boys followed him there, sticks in their hands too. The girls who were cutting grass nearby also came and stood around.

Thatha was all smiles. Holding the dangling snake aloft he told the crowd, 'You call this a snake? It's a mere water-snake. Do you know how many snakes like this I caught when I was your age?'

'How many?' asked a boy from the crowd.

'I was even younger than Kandasami then. I would carry three snakes in each hand. I'd whirl them in the air and throw them to the ground. They would just lie there, dazed, as if they were drunk on palm toddy!' As he said this everyone came and sat around him in a circle. The snake coiled itself around Thatha's arm.

'Thatha, let's see you whirling this snake now and throwing it to the ground!' said Kandasami.

'Okay, look here now. Please make way, make more space.' Thatha took hold of the snake's tail and started whirling it in the air. Then he threw it far away.

The boys gazed at him in amazement. Thatha laughed. 'Looking at me like this for such a small feat? If you listen to what I tell you now, you will be struck dumb!'

Immediately everyone started pleading, 'Thatha, please tell us. Thatha, let us hear it!'

Thatha sat down and everyone settled down around him.

'Those days my father would graze the cattle in the Karuvelangadu forest on the west. I used to go with him. One day, I found a snake hanging from a karuvelam tree.

'How big was the snake, Thatha?'

'A beeeeeg snake! My body tingled with fear but I went near and took a look. Unkappanoli! The snake had a sparrow in its mouth!'

'Do snakes eat sparrows, Thatha?'

'No, they don't, they just look at them and let them go away! What a fool you are! Why only sparrows, they can even swallow our fowl!'

'What did you do then, Thatha? Did you save the sparrow?' asked Kandasami.

'I looked around. I thought hard about how best to save it. Saw a piece of clay lying nearby. Picked it up, gave a mighty swing, and it went and hit the snake right on its head. The snake dropped the sparrow and slithered away. "You think you can escape after killing an innocent sparrow? Here's more for you!" I aimed at the snake twice more. It was hit, but escaped with its life. Then I picked up the sparrow and left.'

'What then, Thatha? Was it still alive?'

'How can anything that goes into a snake's mouth survive? I took it to my father and showed it to him. He asked me to throw it away.'

'Where did you throw it, Thatha?'

'I didn't throw it, da! I dug a hole under the tree and buried it. Poor sparrow! Its body was covered with blood. After that, whenever I passed that way, I would pluck flowers—some erikkampoo, thuthippoo and manjanathippoo—and place them on the sparrow's grave.'

'If we go now will we see that grave, Thatha?'

'How will you? Didn't I bury it when I was your age? How can it still be around?'

'Another time, I beat a big water-snake to death and was playing around with it, when a pot-bellied Naicker came that way. Know what I did? I swung the snake round and round in the air and deliberately let it go and fall on him! You should have seen him run with his pot-belly jiggling up and down! It was so funny!'

He glanced back at the cattle and exclaimed, 'Elaika! The cattle have all gone into the crops. Run! Get them out! Run!' He stood up and started walking away quickly. The boys rushed ahead of him to herd the cattle away, but while they were doing that the owner of the fields arrived. The boys took fright and ran, slipping on the bunds, falling, getting up and running again.

'How can you be so irresponsible? You call yourself an old man? You goaded the young fellows on and let the cattle stray into the crops! Be careful or I'll break your buffalo's legs,' roared the landlord. Thatha went and got his buffalo back.

The boys were all watching from a distance, unhappy at Thatha's sorry plight. Why couldn't he have run away to the other side, why did he keep standing where he was?

Thatha spoke up fearlessly, 'Ayya, have your crops been destroyed? We shooed the cattle away before they could enter the field. Why are you shouting yourself hoarse like this?'

'I was there, so you came running and shooed the cattle away. But if I'm not around you will let the cattle loose in the crops. I know you, you thieving dogs!'

'You, don't you *dare* abuse us! Born just yesterday—how dare you call me a thieving dog? I'll wring your neck, aama!' shouted Thatha as he drove his buffalo along. The landlord yelled back furiously.

When Thatha reached them, the boys asked, 'Are you not frightened at all, Thatha? Talking to landlords like that! We were so scared that he would beat you up.' It was Kandasami who spoke.

'It's chaps like you who fart and run away at the sight of landlords. What do I have to fear from this lowly fellow?'

'You are a grown-up, that's why you're not afraid. If it was small kids, he would have beaten them up.'

'You think so? Take a look in our cheri. Even grown men, seeing the landlords, remove the towels from their shoulders, wind them around their waists and bow deeply. Fellows with moustaches pee down their legs with fear. Even when I was your age, I wasn't scared. My father would shout at me because I had no fear.'

As they came away, driving the cattle, Thatha spoke again. 'When my father grazed the villagers' cattle, the landlord's cattle would also be there, le? So, whoever had abused my father or me, I would ride only that fellow's cattle. There used to be a landlord named Kovaalan then, I named his cow Kovaalan and rode only that cow! "Elay, Kovaala, go east, da! Come here, da! Go there, da!" I would make it sweat terribly, imagining that I was riding that landlord! Even my father would plead with me not to ride the landlord's cattle, but I wouldn't listen.' Having recounted this, he fell silent for some time. The boys, too, asked no more questions.

'Why are you so silent?' demanded Thatha. 'You should never fear another person without reason. Does he have horns on his head? He's just a man like us, why should we be scared of him?'

'Yes, Thatha, we shouldn't be scared,' said Kandasami. 'People like him fart into our mouths if we're afraid of them.'

'Do you know in what ways they abused my father? But he wouldn't say a word, tolerated all their abuse. But I refuse to leave it at that, I will even shit on the landlord's cattle.'

'What is it to them if you shit on their cattle, Thatha?'

'Didn't I give the cattle his name? I'd call out his name and start shitting!'

'What would you do after that, Thatha?'

'Say that, for some reason, I had to go with my father to the landlords' houses. They wouldn't let us enter. Do you know what I did? I threw cow-dung at their doors! My father would be trembling with fright,' said Thatha, laughing uproariously.

'Did they see you throwing the dung, Thatha?'

'What if they did? Would they tear my hair out? One

of them did see and started shouting. My father pleaded with him, saying I was only a small child, I hadn't done it on purpose, and so on. I ran off without so much as looking back...Seri, let's go home now.' And Thatha drove the buffalo homewards. The boys did the same.

But on the way Thatha again said, 'You know that Komaravel Naicker? He beat up my father once. Beat him, saying the cattle didn't return home. But his cow had wandered away somewhere and returned much later. Anger went straight to my head. You know what I did? I grabbed my father's grazing-stick and just let that cow have it, whack, whack, whack! The fellow came running after me, my father ran with him. I said, "The beating your cow got today, you yourself will get tomorrow, you Naicker! I won't rest till I give you blow for blow, dei!"'

'"Ayyaiyyo! You called a Naicker "Dei"?'

'Naicker or Noicker, who cares! If he hits us for no reason we must hit back, or he will think we are easy to exploit.'

Thatha was about to enter his street when Eenjediyan appeared.

'What is it, Eenjediyan? Why are you in such a hurry? Can't you stay in one place? Dragging yourself around with your crooked legs!' said Thatha.

One of Eenjediyan's legs was slightly crooked so he leaned to one side while walking. He looked at the buffalo and said, 'How is it, Malandi, that the buffalo hasn't delivered yet? Did that Rajaram Ayya come and demand it against the loan?'

'He'll demand, will he? And will I just give it away

when he comes and asks? I have paid him a thousand rupees so far for a two-hundred-rupee loan. Now I have to give the buffalo also? Let that thieving motherfucker come—I will ask the buffalo to pee in his mouth!' shouted Malandi angrily.

All eyes were riveted to Thatha. 'Let him come!' he shouted again, 'I will decide one way or another. I don't care about this stupid life. How long can we go on being cheated by them, go on letting them cheat us?'

'Even if a bullock delivers a calf, this Malandi fellow will never change,' said Eenjediyan, and he left.

Malandi stood alone in the middle of the street, roaring in anger, 'That Vadhyar Naicker, how do you think he got the name Hanging-Intestines Naicker? When I was a little boy, unkappanoli, that fellow called me a Parayar. I made his cow lunge at him and slit his belly in two! I made his own cow tear him apart! That was when I stopped grazing the village cattle. Looks like that Rajaram also wants his intestines torn out now. I'll keep the buffalo's horns nicely sharpened, let the scoundrel come to claim the buffalo! Just let him!'

The Ichi Tree Monkey

Whenever she went near an Arasa tree, memories of her village would come rushing to Parvathi's mind. In her village, it was called the Ichi tree. The paddy threshing square was under it. Parvathi could not help laughing to herself even now when she thought of how, during her elementary school vacations, she would go to the threshing ground to sweep up the leftover paddy and barter it at the Nadar's shop for sweet potato. How she relished that!

Near the threshing ground was the cemetery of the Bible folks. The kids at school used to whisper, 'Don't go near the threshing ground at noon. That's the time when the ghosts and ghouls from the cemetery come to rest on the Ichi tree.' One day, when she happened to be there, a strong wind blew. The Ichi tree swayed furiously in the wind and its fruit fell on the ground in heaps. She gathered them up in her skirt and brought them to the village kids. But they were cowardly asses. Not a single girl accepted the fruit. Instead, they tried to scare her.

'Ei, Parvathi, don't eat the fruit. The demons on the Ichi tree are the ones shaking the branches, dancing on them and causing all the fruit to fall. Don't eat the fruit they dropped. Your belly will swell up and you'll die.' How could anyone eat it after hearing such dire things? Immediately, a pit was dug and the fruit was buried... Now, she felt like laughing at those foibles.

Parvathi became a teacher after completing her studies. The Ichi tree stood right on the way to the school. Soaring up from the ground, it touched the skies. A monkey family had taken up residence on it. Every day, Parvathi spent five minutes watching the monkeys on the tree before proceeding to school. It wasn't just her, the entire gang of school kids stopped there, called out to the monkeys and played with them before going to school. As soon as the kids called out 'Rama Rama', monkey after monkey came down the tree. Parvathi wondered how a monkey knew that his name was being called. Later, she understood. The monkey did not come down because he was called Rama, but because of the biscuits, vadais and other eatables the kids had in their hands. The children always brought something for the monkeys, without fail. For them, the monkey was a god. They were told so at home.

It was a daily feast for the monkeys. As soon as they heard 'Rama Rama' they came and ate up everything and had a jolly good time. As if that wasn't enough, there was the fruit the Ichi tree bore. The monkeys polished off all the fruit. They scared off the sparrows who came near. The monkeys lorded it over that tree. How high-handed they were! On a branch that forked into two smaller ones, resting its back against one branch and its legs on the other, a monkey would watch the people passing by underneath and bare its teeth in a grimace. Sometimes the monkeys jumped from branch to branch, creating much mayhem. The entire tree would start shaking. Parvathi liked to be there. On the way to and from school, she always spent some time under the tree. It was a lovely sight to watch a baby monkey hang on to its mother's breast and suck on its nipples. In between suckling, it raised its head and looked here and there. It was so cute!

But this idyllic state had only existed till last week. The kids had now started driving away the monkeys. Two days ago, returning from school, Parvathi had found a gang of kids standing under the tree and stoning the monkeys. She asked them why they were doing so. An old man passing by also asked them the same, 'Aei! Why stone them? The poor dumb, mouthless creatures!'

'Mouthless? Look at them. They have mouths to eat sugar. Thieving monkeys!' one kid shouted angrily.

Parvathi asked, 'My dear, what did they do?'

'Teacher, Valliyakka bought two kilos of sugar from the fair price shop and came this way. That big monkey snatched the bag of sugar from her just like that! It scooped up all the sugar and ate it!'

Parvathi looked up at the branch he pointed to. Instead of getting angry, she felt like laughing. The monkey was sitting on the highest branch with the yellow bag in one hand, gulping down the sugar with the other palm. Half the sugar reached its mouth, while the rest spilled down in a stream. Underneath, the spilt sugar lay all around the tree.

'Why did Valliyakka let go of the bag?'

'They came down stealthily and snatched it, Teacher. How many snacks we have fed these monkeys, Teacher! Still they behave this way. They're thieving monkeys, Teacher!'

Parvathi was speechless. But she did not feel anger as she watched the monkeys eating the sugar. She could only enjoy the sight. She left without saying anything further. After that, the monkeys lost all the kids' respect. The monkeys now seemed cheerless.

Two or three days later, when Parvathi passed that way, the monkeys were not to be seen. She thought that the kids must have driven them away altogether. But soon she spied a monkey riding on the back of a fat pig a little distance from the tree. Parvathi stood transfixed, as the monkey rode the pig quite majestically and ceremoniously, turning its head hither and thither as if leading some big procession. She was overwhelmed with mirth and astonishment. She stood there for some time even after the monkey and the pig had vanished into the underbrush. She thought of it the whole day. On returning in the evening, she again saw the monkey riding the pig. But she could not watch for long as the kids went after them, throwing stones to drive them away. Parvathi got angry with the kids and shouted at them. But her shouts fell on deaf ears.

'Dei! That thieving monkey is riding the pig. Don't let it get away!'

'The pig is your friend? Wait and see what we are going to do to you and the pig.'

'Elei! Look, the monkey is lowering its head to the pig and telling him something!'

Shouting, the kids chased them away. Though the pig ran fast, the monkey never slipped off. The monkey disappeared, riding on the back of the pig.

Parvathi felt bad. On her way home, she was preoccupied thinking of this incident...

'Dear pig, look at these kids! Till recently, they called me "Rama" with respect and gave me things to eat. Now look how they abuse me, screaming "monkey, monkey!"' It was the monkey, speaking sadly.

The pig laughed a little and snorted, 'Well, *aren't* you a monkey? Then why mind being called one?'

'If they had always called me a monkey, I wouldn't mind. You must have observed how they used to call out "Rama, Rama" to me. It hurts when they call me just a monkey now.'

The pig teased him, 'Yes, if they were very fond of you till recently, I wonder why they drive you away now.'

'As if you know nothing! One can't trust these human kids at all. Didn't I snatch a bag of sugar from a woman the other day? Since then, they have turned into enemies.'

'Was it right, what you did? Finished off two kilos of that poor woman's sugar!'

'No, I had barely a mouthful. The rest was spilled.'

'In any case, what you did was wrong. They called you "Rama" and gave you things to eat, but you went and did such a thing. You didn't live up to the respect they gave you.'

As the pig said this, the monkey became angry.

With his front paw he knocked the pig on the head and said, 'Why are you defending them? Did they call me "Rama" for no reason? Do you know how my ancestor helped their Lord Rama? Why do you think they call us Anjaneyar and worship us?'

'How do you know all this?'

'My Paatti told me. That's how I know.'

'And my grandmother used to tell me how the Lord once took *our* form.'

Before the pig had even finished saying this, the monkey clapped his hands and laughed. 'Don't talk such nonsense to anyone else! They'll make mince-meat out of you!'

'Why? You speak about your own exalted status, can't I also make a similar claim?' The pig was irritated.

'You mean you and I are equal? Don't talk rubbish,' the monkey shouted in excitement.

'Of course it isn't rubbish. I can't blame you, though. How would you know about how the Lord incarnated as a pig?' the pig grunted.

'I know, I know. So what? Does that make us equal?'

'You are right. We can't be equals. I'm a step higher than you. Know why? You only *helped* the Lord. But the Lord *himself* took our form. Whose status is higher, then? Tell me.' Saying this, the pig laughed haughtily, like a villain.

When he laughed thus, the monkey almost lost his grip and fell off. Dragging himself up by the pig's ears, he regained his posture. In a less angered voice, he said, 'Yes, all this is true. But, if we look at the way people treat you, you don't get the esteem and respect that I get. They will never respect you.'

'Why not?'

'Because you roam around in garbage mounds, eating foul stuff. You also don't look presentable or dignified. They simply can't bear the sight of you, especially your snouty face!'

'Hey, how about *your* bloody face? When all is said and done, you are just like those humans. They are the ones bothered about dark skin, fair skin, beauty, ugliness, purity and impurity. Shame! They even make distinctions among themselves as male and female and fight with each other. By speaking like them you have exposed your vile nature. They say that humans descend from you. They must be right.' Saying this, with a great shrug, the pig pushed the monkey to the ground.

Regaining his balance quickly, the monkey stood in the pig's path, blocking his way. 'Look, you can abuse me all you want, but don't connect me to those humans. That makes me furious. We are *not* like them. Just look at their faces, always tense. They don't smile or express joy—not even a wee bit. These school kids keep going this way and that. Look at their faces. Like a monkey who chewed some ginger…Oops! Ignore that—I've mentioned my own self!… I mean, look at their faces, always unhappy…at least when they see us, they laugh, they play. Otherwise they just carry loads of books… Poor things!'

'They go to study, that's why,' the pig suggested.

'What if they are studying? Do they have to carry such

heavy burdens, like donkeys? Good thing we were not born as humans. Or else, we would also be like them, wandering around helpless, always in pain.' The monkey once again scrambled up and sat on the pig's back.

'If the kids are like this, what shall I say about their elders? They run around earning money. What for? They have no happiness. Have you seen Parvathi Teacher passing this way? You can see so much sorrow on her face. The moment she approaches this tree, she starts laughing when she sees us. How pretty she looks then! Just to see her happy and looking so pretty, we perform tricks. She likes that.'

While they were engaged in conversation thus, the mate and baby of the monkey came rushing over. The monkey leapt down from the pig's back and started running with them. The three of them scampered quickly up a palm tree nearby. They began to play, leaping from one tree to the other. The pig, now joined by its piglets, laughed aloud and they all rushed away from there like an army.

'How did I get lost in such weird thoughts?' Parvathi wondered and heaved a big sigh.

Stereotype

The summer vacation was over. School reopened, as usual, on the first of June. Kalaivani always enjoyed going to the school. She loved the children, especially the new ones admitted to the first standard. For the last twenty years, Kalaivani had worked as a teacher for first-standard kids. She understood the mental and emotional strain on kids newly admitted to school. When children who had till then happily roamed around free were trapped within four walls, they rebelled, and Kalaivani always sympathized with them. Some sat outside the class room and put up a struggle, refusing to come inside. Attempts to coax them in, using many methods, did not always work. Even if they were left outside, they only waited for an opportune moment to run back home. This situation carried on for at least two months.

This year was no different. When a boy named Vettrichelvan was asked to come into the class room, he said, 'You keep going out and coming in when you like. Why am I told to remain inside?' Then he lay down on the floor outside the class. Some kids who were already sitting inside were weeping piteously. Some of them had begun to shed copious tears as soon as they entered the school compound. Whenever Kalaivani had to pick up the little children and shut them inside the class room, she felt distressed. She remembered the bite that a girl named Nancy had given her when she was carried inside. Kalaivani had tried to seat her on the table forcefully and stop her from crying. The girl had continued to cry bitterly and thrown the plastic box in her hand to the floor. When Kalaivani had picked up all the scattered slate and wooden pencils and tamarind seeds and put them back in the box and given it to the girl, she had accepted it, but had continued to cry, saying, 'There is a slate pencil on the floor.' Kalaivani could not help laughing whenever she remembered that scene. If any of these new children had an elder sister or brother in a senior class, they would go and sit happily with them. They felt safe then.

Kalaivani now introduced herself to the class and asked the children their names. Some gave their names enthusiastically, some mumbled, and some said nothing. When she asked a girl who had her thumb in her mouth, she took it out briefly, said 'Bujji' and put her thumb back into her mouth. Kalaivani asked her again,

'What name did you say?'

'Bujji.'

'Oh, Bujji?'

'Not "Oh Bujji", Just Bujji,' The girl corrected her firmly. Kalaivani wanted to laugh, but did not.

'Not Bujji, Teacher, Bajji...Plantain Bajji,' a boy named Kumar said and laughed.

Bujji stared at him furiously.

'Okay, now you tell me, kid.'

'See...I have two names. One is Bujji...the other is Swetha,' she said, lisping.

Kalaivani did not hear clearly what she said. She asked again,

'What was that? Swetha?'

'You don't know even this much? Bujji when I am at home. Swetha when I am in school. My mother told me that.'

'Bujji can touch her nose with her tongue, Teacher,' Kavya informed her.

'Really, Bujji? Let me see you doing it.'

'Do it, Bujji. How many times you did it at home!' Kavya said.

'Kavya, are you and Bujji from the same village?' Kalaivani asked.

'See...me and Bujji are relatives. Her father is my Chittappa. My father is her Periappa. No, Bujji? Now, touch your nose with your tongue.' As soon as Kavya said this, Bujji stuck out her tongue and easily touched her nose with its tip. Everyone clapped and laughed. She also laughed joyfully.

'Bujji, you look so small. Have you turned five?'

'Mmm...yes. I can touch my ear with my hand.' She raised her right hand, twisted it around her back and touched her left ear. The first bell rang just then. Bujji picked up her bag and ran out. Kalaivani ran after her and brought her back.

'This bell is not for going home. Only when the bell rings for a long time can you go home, understood?'

Before she finished, Bujji asked, 'When will the long-bell ring?'

'At four,' Kalaivani informed her. After that, every ten minutes, Bujji asked the time. Kalaivani kept telling her it was not yet four. Soon, Bujji pursed her lips and started crying.

Kalaivani asked Kumar to go and bring Bujji's elder brother, Ashok, who was in the fourth standard. As soon as Ashok arrived, Bujji ran to him and clutched his hand. He held her hand and started crying too.

'Now, why are *you* crying? Only your sister is new to school. She is a kid. What about you? You also cry when your sister cries?'

'I want to go home, Teacher. I want to see my mother, Teacher. I want to be with her, Teacher,' Kalaivani was surprised as Ashok kept saying this and crying.

'Dei! Why are you talking like this? You were with your mother for one month in the holidays. You have studied here from the first standard. Your sister is new here. She is a small kid. Why is a big boy like you crying? Tell me.'

'Teacher, during the holidays…their father died. That's why they are crying. Their father drank a lot and died. They say my father will die next. Is it not so, Ashok Anna?' Kavya said, as if it was the most common thing in the world.

'Why are you talking like this?'

'You know why? My father too drinks a lot. That's why my Paatti said that he will also die soon, Teacher.'

'My mother is alone at home, Teacher. That's why I want to leave,' Ashok said.

'Is your mother a young kid? She is a grown-up person. She can be alone. Stop crying now and study. Only then will your sister stop crying.'

'Since my father died, I have to look after her, Teacher. I have to go home, Teacher. I have to take care of my mother. Let this baby sit here and study. I will be with my mother and do some work, Teacher.'

'It is your mother who has to take care of you. What work can you do to take care of her? You should study well and get a big job and earn good money to take care of your mother, understood?'

'No, Teacher. I should be with my mother now. Or else, my mother will go to work with other men and become spoiled.' Saying this, he began to whine loudly. Kalaivani was amazed at this.

His small figure, his tiny eyes that protruded slightly and from which tears welled up and flowed, the sadness that swam in them, the little black face that was withstanding so much suffering—Kalaivani took all this in and was dumbstruck. She couldn't quite fathom his pain. She finally spoke. 'Okay, Ashok. You bring your mother along tomorrow. I will talk to her and decide, understood?'

He nodded his head in agreement.

When Kalaivani reached school the next day, Ashok's mother stood there waiting for her. After asking her about Ashok's father's death, Kalaivani told her what Ashok had said the other day. Immediately, Ashok's mother started weeping. Watching her, Ashok also began to weep. Kalaivani was astounded by what his mother then narrated, in between sobs.

'Teacher, this boy is enough to put me to shame. His father, when he was alive, doubted my virtue and beat and kicked me daily and tortured me. That drunkard drank his way to death in a short time. I am at a loss as to how I can bring up these two kids, educate them and make them succesful. To make things worse, from the day his father died, this boy has been talking about me like this constantly and humiliating me. He was all right when he remained home. But from the moment I asked him to go to school, he has been behaving like this. He says he will stay with me and protect me from other men. Is that how boys his age talk, Teacher? When my own son, born from my womb, is saying such cheap things about me, what am I to do? Teacher? How can I take care of these kids without going to work with other men? How can I educate them? He says I should go to work only with women. This fellow, born yesterday, is laying down rules for me. I can only do the work that is offered to me. Am I in a position to choose whether to work with men or women?' She cried miserably as she said this.

'Who stays with you at home now?'

'No one. After sending both kids off to school, I go to assist a mason.'

'You should not do that work. You should not work with men. You should not talk to men. I will come with you. Take me with you! I won't study! Take me to work, Amma!' Ashok howled.

'You see that, Teacher? Did you hear what he said? I think his father's ghost has possessed him. Only after his father died has he started talking like this…The fellow remained a dumb ass as long as his father was alive…In a way, I feel sorry for him, Teacher. In another way, I get so angry with him. What can I do with him?' she cried inconsolably.

Kalaivani had no answer. In the last twenty years, she had never come across a boy like this. Ashok had been studying in the same school for three years. Now, suddenly, he seemed so different. He was acting as if he was an adult.

Ashok's mother said it was time for her to get to work and turned to leave. In a flash, he caught hold of her sari and wouldn't let go. She started beating him. Restraining her, Kalaivani said,

'Okay, Ashok. Let your mother go to work just for today. You concentrate on your studies. She is a grown-up person, no one can do anything to her. She can protect herself.' Then she added, 'Even if you are with your mother, what can you do to protect her? Are you not a small child?'

He bellowed angrily, 'I may be a small child, but I am a *man*!'

Single

Illamalli was a carefree girl; chubby and round like a pumpkin, with good features. She must have been five or six years old. She used to roam around in her street just like the other kids who didn't go to school. Her father and mother were daily-wagers, they left for work at daybreak and returned only after the sun had set. So it was Illamalli who looked after her brother, who was just one-and-a-half years old, and did all the house chores, besides collecting water from the public tap and storing it daily. She also gathered firewood to burn in the oven. On seeing her, the women of the village marvelled: 'This girl drinks only kanji like the other kids, from a mud pot, then how is she so buxom, as if she has already reached puberty?'

'Her mother did not conceive for years after she was born. Being an only child for a time, this girl ate up everything all alone...that's why she's like a millstone already.'

'No, her whole clan is like that. Look at her grandmother. Look at her mother. All bloated up with useless fat.'

'If she took a bath every day and made up her face, she would look like an upper-caste girl.'

'When she actually attains puberty, there's going to be a long line of suitors in front of her home to claim her hand.'

Listening to all this gossip, Illamalli's mother would say, 'God has been gracious enough to give us such fine and healthy children. But what a pity that we don't have the means to bring them up in a decent way. What can we do?'

Seven or eight girls of the same age as Illamalli roamed around with her always, carrying their younger siblings at their waists. All of them went about everywhere as one gang. One day, around three in the afternoon, this gang of kids went to the waterway to the south of the village to relieve themselves. All the women usually used that place to shit, going there either before sunrise or after sunset. The waterway was close to the irrigation tank and during the day, the men of the locality would keep walking up and down that way. The women could not squat there then. That day, Illamalli and her gang who had gone there to defecate squatted in a circle and told stories to each other. In between, they also plucked the thuthi flowers from the fence nearby, gathering them in their skirts and sucking the nectar from them. After defecating at one spot, they shifted to squat at another spot.

The pigs that came to eat the mounds of shit would always fight among themselves, and Illamalli and the others watched the skirmish fearfully before lifting their skirts and moving a little to squat at a different spot. The pigs followed them and waited for the moment when the girls would lift their bums again. When they did not get up for a long time and kept talking to each other, the pigs lost patience and came closer to them, grunting angrily. A huge pig came up behind Illamalli and gave her a push with its snout, causing her to fall forward, and started eating the shit. Scared, Illamalli picked up a stone and hurled it at the pig. The furious pig charged at her, threw itself on her chest, and bit her deeply. Illamalli wore no top, so the flesh on her right breast was torn badly. Blood began to gush from it.

Illamalli screamed, unable to bear the pain. She ran back to her street, still screaming. The other scared kids followed her into the village. The women who saw them, were at loss as to what to do and began to shout comments, seeking more details from each other.

'The bastards, see how they rear their pigs! The little ones can't go out and squat. It's that Muniyandi's pig that's doing all this mischief. We can't let it be now. We should kill it with stones.'

'The wretched creature! It bit her exactly on the breast. Who knows if it will grow back again.'

'Okay, let's not waste time sitting around talking. Let's take her to a doctor. Look how the blood is streaming!" Veeramma said.

'But her mother and father aren't back yet.'

'You good-for-nothing, if we wait till they come back the child will lose all her blood and die,' Veeramma said. Beckoning to Selvaraj who was passing that way, she asked him to carry the girl to the doctor and went along with him. The other women followed.

'Some widow must have cast her evil eye on the girl. Otherwise, why would that killer pig leave all the other girls alone and choose this one to bite?'

'This isn't about some evil eye or any such thing! One should never go anywhere near the waterway in the afternoon. It's the time when ghosts come out. A ghost can appear in the form of a pig.'

'She talks as if she has seen one! There is no such thing as a ghost. Such loose talk will only prevent people from moving about freely.'

Each woman had an opinion and spoke it out as they all walked behind the bleeding girl. They showed her to Doctor Gurumoorthy at the bazaar, but he said the case was beyond him. While they were thinking of getting an ox cart ready to take her to the government hospital, her father and mother returned from work. As soon as she heard what had happened, Illamalli's mother began to wail.

'I knew it was a bad omen when a crow pecked me on the head in the fields. Now look what has happened, just as I had feared! God, what money will I have to spend to get her well again? A whore reared a pig to bite my daughter.'

When the ox cart was ready, they took the girl to the government hospital in the next village. The piece of flesh that was hanging off her was cut away. She was given an injection and the wound was bandaged. It took many days for the wound to heal, and when it was healed, there was nothing like a breast to be seen on the right side of her bosom. Only a scar remained.

After seven or eight years, Illamalli's left breast grew bigger. But on the right side, there was only the scar. And now her mother grew sadder than ever. She was distressed that, because of the pig, her daughter had become a one-breasted woman.

As the years went by, Illamalli also became sad and started worrying. When she attained puberty, people on her street had guffawed, asking if the 'single-breast' had come of age. Eventually, everyone had started calling her 'Single.' Her name, Illamalli, simply vanished, only 'Single' remained. She became furious whenever someone referred to her as 'Single' and would abuse anyone who teased her in that manner. So, just for the fun of seeing her get worked up, people kept calling her 'Single'.

Even four or five years after Single attained puberty, no one came asking for her hand. Other girls her age had all got married and had kids. Only our Single, poor thing, remained at home.

*What if one breast is missing? Don't I also have desires? I want to get married, too, like all the others. I want to bear children and bring them up on my milk. But it seems it is my fate to remain alone like this till I die...*Illamalli thought this often, with much sorrow.

'What can we do about it, child? How many children go to the waterway, but God had written this fate only on your forehead! Please don't lose heart. There must be a man somewhere who is born for you,' her mother consoled her.

Years passed rapidly. Single turned thirty. Though she was resigned to her fate of never being married, whenever she came across other women who were, she was distressed. Meanwhile, her father and mother died. Her younger brother got married. Single bought a milch cow to support herself.

Every day she gathered grass for the cow and fed it. The cow became her only companion. People even nicknamed it 'Single's cow.' She tolerated all this. One day, she went to the field on the western side of the village where beans were grown and the grass was abundant. The owner came to watch her.

'What's this, Single? You've come alone to cut grass? Looking after a milch cow, eh? So how much milk does she give?' he taunted her.

'Call me Single-Dingle and you'll get a mouthful from me. Why are you bothered how much milk the cow squirts? Mind your own bloody business and get lost,' she said angrily.

'What makes you so angry? It was nothing new, what I called you. Your own people call you that.'

'My people may call me anything. Who are *you* to call me so? Say that name again and you'll regret it,' she shouted at him and began to cut the grass faster.

'So what will you do if I call you so? Even if you have only a single one, the one you have is pretty good,' he said slyly and, bending down, put his arm around her.

Single became wild. She stood up in an instant, pushed his hand off and tried to run away. But he grabbed her and would not let go.

Single

Single looked around and realized that he was doing this only because he knew no one was around. She raised the sickle with which she was cutting the grass and slashed at his hand. But she lost her aim. The sickle pierced his eye instead. He screamed, wriggling around in pain. Pressing one palm to the eye from which blood streamed, he yelled. Single dropped the grass that she had cut and ran back home.

Seeing her agitated state on returning, her people asked what had happened. She told them, wailing and weeping, what had happened to her as she was cutting grass.

'Why are you crying? These fools will come to their senses only when you do things like this,' Grandmother Lourde said.

The news of how Landlord Naikkar became single-eyed spread through the village like wild fire. From that day onwards, no one called Illamalli 'Single' again.

The Ancharamanippoo Tree

There was no dearth of ghost stories in Ulattharappatti village. And no one knew them better than Paul Raj Thatha. From the youngest kids to the oldest men, everyone huddled together eagerly to listen to his stories. Even grown-up boys stopped to listen for a while before pushing off.

Some would say, 'Ghosts and demons! He should tell these stories only to gullible people. The sort who go around with a flower tucked behind their ear. Look how all these people sit and waste their time listening to him! They're worse than him—he at least has no work other than cooking up fake stories. We don't believe any of them.' Though they said this bravely, there was a strange disquiet that was sown within them. And yet, Paul Raj Thatha told his stories with so much skill, that even though the stories evoked this uncanny fear deep inside people, everyone desired to hear more.

Paul Raj Thatha never narrated a story on demand. The moment had to arrive for him; even if someone pleaded with him, he would not say anything that easily. The ground below the ancharamanippoo, the five-thirty-flower tree growing to the west of the village, was his chosen stage for narration. I don't remember the correct name of the tree. The village calls it by that name because, as if on cue, precisely at five-thirty in the evening the plant puts out blossoms. Sometimes, Military Anthoni, who lived in South Street, bought rum from the military canteen and shared some of it with Thatha. On the days when Thatha drank, his way of narrating the stories was completely different. He was so enthusiastic that he could not remain seated at one spot. He stood up and enacted the story. If needed, he would even sing a song or two. Sometimes, Military Anthoni joined him, enjoying all this. But such occasions were rare.

I am now forty. I have been listening to Thatha's stories since I was a ten-year-old boy. Those days, the very sight of Thatha evoked fear, as if he himself were a ghost. The stories that he told then were even more scary, yet I had a great desire to listen to him.

I remember one story. I had learnt to ride a bicycle, taken on hire, when I was studying in the sixth standard. Although I had tried pedalling a cycle before, cranking and creaking, this was the first time I began hiring a cycle myself. I waited for Saturdays and Sundays to arrive. I saved all the coins that my mother gave me for buying titbits so that I could hire a cycle, and then I would ride it tirelessly on holidays. Finding me riding the cycle non-stop, without even eating, my mother threatened that she would not give me money anymore. But, ultimately, she gave up. In the beginning, my rides were confined to the village, but on one occasion I rode to the next village and came back. In no time, the people who had seen me at the next village informed my father. I wouldn't have cared if they had told my mother. That night, during dinner, my father started shouting at my mother.

'How many times have I told you not to give him any money! Do you know what he did today? He hired a cycle and rode till Konampatti. He was on the road where buses are running, and that too in the evening! No one would even know if this little fellow was run over on the way. Look at his size—if I gave him one kick, he won't need a second one—and look at the kind of things he does! We treat him as a small boy, but he roams around doing such mischief!'

'When did he go to Konampatti? He pedals around only in the village. Some devil's son has told you all this...Did you go to Konampatti?' Amma asked me.

I kept mum and looked at her, wondering whether to say yes or no. But then, my father yelled angrily,

'Look how he is keeping his mouth shut! He is trying hard to say "No". Just you lie and I will strangle you!'

'Tell us. What do you mean by keeping your mouth shut?'

I nodded my head, indicating 'Yes'.

'You really went there? On a cycle? You went and came back all by yourself? Watching out for the buses, in control of yourself, you pedalled smoothly all the way there and came back? That's not bad at all! Did you ride alone?'

'No, your son rode in a procession with ten people escorting him! If you talk to him like this, he will not stop

The Ancharamanippoo Tree

at Konampatti but carry on till Kuppampatti. All this is because you are lenient with him. Instead of disciplining him, you are all excited, as if he has achieved something great. Look at the fellow. Scared stiff a moment ago, but all alert now, with eyes wide open! One day you're going to get it from me. Don't think you can fool me like you do your mother, understood?'

I barely escaped that day. At night, before going to sleep, I told Amma in detail about my cycle ride to Konampatti and back. Amma was happy. But she warned me not to take that route after sunset. When I asked her why, she said that there was a ghost on the lone palm tree by the side of the road. I listened quietly, but wondered to myself how no ghost had appeared there when I rode past.

It was the day after that, that Paul Raj Thatha narrated the story of the ghost who rode on his cycle. I remember the story as clearly as if I had heard it yesterday. Many people were assembled, as usual, under the five-thirty-flower tree. I and four or five of my classmates huddled right in front of Thatha as he began:

'It so happened that last new moon day, I went on some work beyond the Chathuragiri Hills to the north. See, there was a cattle market that day in that village. Because my old woman and I were just idling away, our elder son asked us to rear a good milch cow. The old woman also started nagging me about it. Unable to stand her nagging, I decided to go and look for one in the market. Hiring a cycle and gulping down some gruel, I started the journey early in the morning.'

'You went on a cycle? You know how to ride one?' It was me who asked.

Thatha looked at me and laughed. Wiping his grey moustache, he said, 'Look at you, big-mouthed brat! You ask me whether I can ride a cycle? Ask your father. He will tell you where all I rode my cycle when I was of a younger age than you. I had to just touch the pedal with my foot and the cycle would fly. Understood, son of Rajendran?'

'Big cycle or small cycle, Thatha?'

'Big one, da! If you sat on it, you could not reach the pedal with your feet. So I stood and pedalled long distances.'

'Seri, leave the cycle-riding story. Come back to the main story,' someone from the crowd said and Thatha returned to the story.

'This is not just a story, like you imagine. This really happened. It was noon by the time I reached that village. I could not pedal as fast as before. Had to take a break here and there and chew on a betel leaf before resuming. On reaching, I went and had a look at the cows. A good milch cow costs ten or twenty rupees, you know! Who can buy a cow at such a high price?'

Thatha took a break and stuffed some tobacco into his mouth.

The boy Mani, who was sitting next to me, asked, 'Cows are available for ten-twenty rupees, Thatha? If so, you should have driven one over here!'

Hearing that, all the elders had a good laugh. Thatha quipped that Mani was a kid speaking like a kid, and resumed his storytelling.

'The afternoon glare was splitting my skull. Thinking that if I rode back in that glare I would faint and fall somewhere and there would be no way to inform the old woman at home, I spread my towel under the huge neem tree on the south side of that village and lay down. The breeze under the neem tree was so cooling that I slept till evening. Around four, the sound of the boys milking the cows and the clanging of the milk cans woke me up. Washing my hands, legs and face at the street handpump, I had a small tea from the teashop nearby and, tying the towel around my head, started pedalling back. Did not stop anywhere. Aiming to reach our village before darkness fell, I pedalled fast. I had covered almost half the distance. People were returning home after finishing the day's labour. Slowly, darkness began to fall. Fortunately, the headlight on the cycle was working. Though I am old, my eyesight is still good. I was riding the cycle, when suddenly there was the figure of a woman with a baby in her arms standing in front of me. I kept my eyes on the road and kept pedalling, ringing the bell. As I rode on, the woman always remained in front, at a constant distance. She was neither receding nor coming towards me! Then I managed to regain my composure. Seri, this is that ass, I realized.'

'Which ass, Thatha?'

'Elai! Just shut up. What then, Thatha?'

'What then! I had to manage the situation and somehow reach home. I took a decision: whatever happened, I would not stop pedalling or get off the cycle. Then I started pedalling as fast as I could. After some time, she vanished from view. Could she wag her tail at me? How many such apparitions I have seen! But one should never have fear. Fear is our number one enemy...Now, thinking that the wretched one was gone, I pedalled in a relaxed manner. I must have been one mile away from our village. But however forcefully I pedalled, the cycle was not moving fast. It was as if I was riding with four or five sacks of paddy on the back carrier. It was so difficult. Wondering why the cycle was so heavy, I turned to glance at the back and...oh...it was such a blood-curdling sight that my innards were shaken.'

We small kids became shit scared and huddled closer to Thatha. The others did not move a muscle and stood frozen. Thatha too did not speak for some time. As he remained motionless, our fear increased. After some time, it was Nasu Annachi who bravely asked Thatha what happened.

'Elai, if I say this you will not believe me. That wretched woman was sitting on the carrier with the child! I was utterly shocked for a moment. But I did not stop pedalling the cycle even once. However heavy it was, I kept pedalling. When I reached the paddy field of Chandrasekhar Ayya, suddenly there was the sound of someone falling into the well nearby. At the same moment, the weight was lifted off the cycle and it began to move as fast. Only then did I understand. That was the boundary of that wretched ghost. You know, all ghosts have their own boundary. They never cross it. Without looking back, I rode on and reached home. I informed only the old woman at home of what had happened that day. Know what she told me? The daughter of the owner of that field, who was pregnant, had fallen into that well and died. It seems many people have sighted her blocking their paths with a baby in her arms.'

'Ei Thatha! Even if you are spinning a yarn, do it so we can believe you. How can a ghost ride on a cycle, Thatha? You told us before that ghosts stay away from iron. Then how can a ghost sit on a cycle? Is the cycle not made of iron?'

'I knew you would ask such questions. That wretched ghost did not sit down on the carrier like we do. She sat six inches above it. She did not touch the carrier at all. She seemed to sit so lightly on the carrier, yet carried so much weight.'

'Did she not touch you while sitting behind you, Thatha?'

'Would she dare touch me? There is a force around me like a fence. It is called courage of the mind. No ghost can touch me. They may come close and try all kinds of tricks, but they cannot overwhelm me.'

'Are you God, then, Thatha?'

'Elai! If you have no fear in your heart, then there is no ghost or any such damned thing. For the fellow who is scared, all dark things are ghosts. God or ghost, they are within our control.'

'Tell us about the time you saw a group of ghosts when you were coming back from some other village.'

'That was close by here. Towards Athipatti village to the west of our village. When my niece's mother-in-law died, everyone paid a funeral visit and all of them returned in the morning itself. I was asked to leave the next day. But I thought that if I left at night, then I could go for some work in the morning. With this in mind, I had my dinner and after chewing on a betel leaf, I started back. The moonlight was bright. I came along the path through the village fields and had crossed the village tank. There is another small village there named Kolaram. There can't be more than a hundred people living there. At that unearthly hour, around midnight, I came across a group of people sitting on a rock and making conversation. I wondered why those people were assembled there at that unholy hour, outside their village. I soon reached the village itself, and met someone along the path. When I asked why around fifty people were gathered on a rock outside, discussing something, and who those people were, the elderly man said, "That's a gathering of ghosts. Many years ago, when there was a caste war in the area, many people were hacked to death. The ones who died gather like this sometimes on the rock. To see them speak, cry and roam around sighing is a sorry sight.'

'After hearing this, my heart grew heavy. The ones who were hacked to death were all from our own community. Many times, I have come across those who died a premature death roaming around like this as ghosts. I don't fear them.'

With sorrow that could not be expressed, and in fear, those who were sitting there got up and left, one by one.

Thatha is unable to walk properly nowadays. Even so, he cannot sit idle in the same spot for long. He keeps loitering and telling stories. I was reminded of all the stories he had told before when I heard the one that was currently in circulation in the village. Now, this story I could neither believe nor disbelieve. I wanted to hear what Thatha had to say about it and so did many others like me. So I went in search of Thatha. I was told that Thatha and Paatti had gone to stay with their son. Everyone was sad that Thatha was not in the village then. But he could not stay away from the village for long. I thought he would come back within two days. And that evening itself, Thatha returned. It was Chinna Rasu who broke the news to Thatha.

'Thatha, last month, on the Konampatti road, there was an accident, did you know that?'

'Is it the same incident where one of our village boys ran a tractor over Bangaru Ayya?'

'The same, Thatha. But our village boy had not run him over. Ayya was fully drunk when he came on a two-wheeler and collided with the tractor and was injured badly in the head. He died on the spot. Now he's been coming as a ghost and possessing a girl from our village. What do you say to that, Thatha?'

'Is it so? What is he saying?'

'Why don't we all go to that girl's house, Thatha? You can see for yourself.'

Everyone went with Thatha to Saroja's house. Saroja sat there with her hair all dishevelled. She must have been around twenty. Her father and mother were sitting in front of her, sunk in sorrow. Only her grandma did the talking.

'Ayya, is it proper, what you are doing? We are coolies surviving by doing labour in your fields. And you have come and possessed a girl from our village! What can we do? We don't have any wealth. Please tell us what you desire, Sami. We will do whatever we possibly can. Accept what we offer and leave this girl, Sami. We are people who struggle even for our daily gruel.'

The ghost who had possessed Saroja spoke: 'I don't need anything grand. Buy a quarter whisky and bring it here. I will go away.'

Saroja's father ran out, came back with the whisky and put the bottle down. Saroja picked it up, opened it and gulped it all down. Everyone was stunned to see this. Thatha had a smile on his face.

Saroja's grandma spoke again. 'Look at your caste and status, Sami! How could you leave all your caste people and come and possess a lower-caste girl like this? When you were alive, you would not even lie down with your head in the direction of this street. A man like you, is it proper for you to come to the house of a lower-caste family? Please leave us, Sami. You will be blessed.'

Saroja shouted in a male voice: 'Don't talk about caste! Only those who are alive have caste, ghosts don't have caste!'

Empty Nest

A pomegranate tree stood in front of the house. Right at the front door, with its branches spread beautifully. The leaves and some tender fruits lay scattered around the doorway. Whether it bore fruits or not, the way that tree bloomed with orange blossoms was a sight to behold.

Though the tree was inside the compound of our house, it was only rarely that we got the fruits, the people who lived nearby would get to them before us. Moreover, squirrels came and devoured the fruits. Paatti, my grandma, had a grudge against the tree as she thought it was just standing there uselessly, adding to the litter with its fallen leaves and not even giving us any fruit worth the name. But I felt otherwise. I liked it a lot. Even my mother had no complaint against it. My home consisted of only the three of us. Me and my mother were in support of the tree. Only my Paatti insisted that it should not have stood in front of the house, it should have been at the back.

'But if it stands at the back, we wouldn't even get to see the flowers.'

'And Christians follow no tradition that distinguishes between the front and the back of the house. We can grow plants wherever we want.'

We said all this to shut the old woman up.

Actually, it wasn't even a proper tree. Though it grew tall, it bent and swayed in any passing breeze, as if it had no wooden-core inside. Even the hibiscus shrub standing next to it did better—however strongly the wind blew, it stood erect, never bending over like the pomegranate tree. A log of wood was fixed to support the pomegranate, since it didn't seem to have the strength to stand straight. Then Madhavan Sir, who lived in the house opposite, advised me that if I also tied it firmly to a branch from the eucalyptus, it would not sway any more. I thought about doing that. But then I remembered the nest built on the tree by a sparrow couple, and decided not to do anything for the time being.

It was a Sunday morning when, sitting in front of the house, reading the newspaper, I heard some chirping sounds. I ignored them and continued reading. Sparrows often came and chirruped on that pomegranate tree. They would soon leave, I thought. When I had finished reading and had folded my newspaper, I looked at the tree and saw two sparrows busily engaged in building a nest. Small sparrows, coffee-brown. Their faces and beaks were black. Beneath the beak, half the neck was white, with little black spots. They were building their nest vigorously and speedily. Watching those sparrows filled me with joy.

Luckily, it was a holiday. I sat as if nailed to the spot. Because there was a compound wall running around the house, I could escape the glances of people outside. They would have irritated me with continuous questions—like, 'What are you watching? What are you doing sitting at the same spot for such a long time?' and so on. Or they would have just stared at me as if I was loony. Even my mother was grumbling about the way I was watching the sparrows without pause. But I hardly cared.

The sparrow couple continued to build the nest all morning. One of them remained on the tree, constructing the nest. The other would fly away and come back with straw in its beak, which it would give to its mate before flying off again. This sparrow flew energetically, without wasting a single second, and brought back more and more straw, while the other one bent the straw according to its wish with its beak and spliced it into the nest, building it into a round shape. It was a pleasure watching it weave the straws into one another. The sparrows continued building their nest till afternoon, and I kept watching them.

I did not pay heed even to my grandma's shouts of 'Why is this girl sitting there watching all this as if she has no other work!' I even finished my lunch hurriedly and came and sat in front of the door again. I don't know if those sparrows ate anything. They continued with their labour, working very fast. I couldn't understand why they were in such a hurry. I thought they wanted to finish building the nest for shelter before the rain fell. Also, that they might be in a hurry to lay eggs.

By afternoon, they had stopped building with straw. One sparrow now flew somewhere to fetch green grass in its beak to continue the nest building. The sparrow was so small. The blade of grass it carried was four or five times longer than itself. As I watched, it did not look as if a sparrow was carrying the grass, but that a long blade of grass was flying by itself! It was no ordinary grass. It was as broad and long as a leaf of sugarcane. I wondered where the sparrow had located it. It looked like the special variety grown as cattle feed. I had never seen it in my locality. This must be an extremely smart sparrow, I thought, to have found this variety. The sparrow on the tree took the long green grass and curved it above the straw-bed like a roof. However fast the sparrow that flew away came back with the grass, the other one matched its pace by building just as fast. The sparrow bringing the grass would whirr away like an arrow from a bow and return at the same speed with another blade of grass, but even before it reached the tree, the other sparrow would have shaped the blade of green grass from the last trip and finished adding it to the roof.

They continued this the whole day. I too did not do any other work. Before evening, they finished building the nest. Then they made an opening for entry and exit. In order that the nest should not get wet, they laid some straw which extended beyond the entrance. Then they came and sat outside, apparently having a conversation.

As if on cue, the very next day, rain fell. The sparrows

stayed inside their nest comfortably. I was sure their nest would withstand the rain. My mother informed me that the female sparrow would now lay eggs, and once the chicks were hatched, they would leave the nest. I did not like the idea that they would leave. But what could I do? I derived some satisfaction from the fact that they would remain there at least till the chicks had hatched.

Watching them became a daily routine for me. Even in the office, I would sometimes think about them. In the evening, I would rush back home to watch them. I spent some time with them before doing any other work at home. Watching those sparrows so happily in conversation every day, I even began to get a bit jealous. I often thought about the freedom, peace, joy and lack of worry with which those two chirruped to each other. For us, building a house is a herculean task. Even when it is built, its maintenance continues to be difficult. It seemed to me that those sparrows had no such worry.

But I soon came to realize that I was wrong.

One day, on returning from office, I found the nest shattered. My anger knew no bounds when I saw it in shreds. I thought it must be the handiwork of my grandma, because the old woman grumbled so much about them.

'Couldn't these cursed sparrows find any other place? They fill the place with so much litter building their nest. However much one sweeps, they keep going out and coming back with grass and dropping it all over the place. Not only grass but also leaves plucked from the tree. And they're always shitting everywhere. How many times can one sweep all that away in a day?'

I had heard Paatti going on like this many times. I went straight to her now and asked her angrily about the ruined nest. But she replied with sorrow and sympathy for the sparrows.

'A good-for-nothing crow came and shredded the nest and went off. The poor sparrows! How much effort they put into building the nest! They took a whole day. But the mad crow wrecked it in a second.'

'What are you saying, Paatti? A crow did it? Don't tell lies, old woman. You wrecked it yourself and you're putting the blame on a crow. All these days there was no crow, how did it suddenly appear? This is your handiwork—you were unhappy that the sparrows littered the place. But those poor sparrows are not going to spare you!'

'Chi chi...you think I'm so stone-hearted? After you leave for office, it is I who takes pleasure in watching them throughout the day. This morning, in front of my very eyes, that rogue crow flew in suddenly and with its beak pulled down all the grass on the nest. Luckily, I was right here. If I hadn't run out and shooed it away with the broom, it would have wrecked the whole nest.'

'Why should the crow come and wreck the nest? Is there a quarrel between the crow and the sparrow?... Poor, innocent creatures, how beautifully they'd made that nest! Look how it has been destroyed. That crow...it was jealous of the sparrows. The crow makes its ugly nest with twigs and thorns...it was jealous. Its heart must have burned at the sight of the pretty nest of the sparrows...' I was inconsolable.

'No, no, the crow did this to peck the eggs of the sparrows and break the shells to eat the yolk,' Paatti said and then added angrily, 'Why should it nourish its body by eating the eggs of these poor little things!'

In sorrow, I stood there staring at the broken nest. Then our neighbour Rasathi came over. Rasathi must have been seven or eight years old. She was studying in the fourth standard in the government school. She also loved those sparrows and frequently came to our house to look at their nest on the pomegranate tree. Whenever we met, she would want to know how they were. Now, finding me standing there sadly, she asked me, 'Why, Aunty, why do you look so sad? Where are the sparrows?'

'A crow came and tore up their nest. The sparrows are gone.'

'Will they never return to this nest now, Aunty?'

'They will, but after some time,' I said.

'How can they? After the crow has pecked their nest, they will never come back. What's the guarantee that the crow that came once will not come again? The sparrows must have left for some other place.'

As Paatti said this, I almost flew into a rage. Just then, Rasathi said, 'Aunty, do you know the sparrow story? My school teacher told it to us.'

I felt that in my disturbed state it would be good to sit down and speak with the girl for a little while. So I asked her to tell me the story. She also sat down and began narrating the story enthusiastically.

'In a village, there was a coconut tree. Many sparrows had made their hanging nests on the coconut leaves.

When they were building the nests, a monkey on the tree began taunting them by saying, "Why are you building a nest with so much effort? Look at me! How happily I live! Instead of enjoying leaping from tree to tree, why bother to build a nest and live on the same old tree forever?"'

'One of the sparrows told the monkey, "The rainy season is approaching. Before that you should also build a nest. Otherwise, you will get wet." On hearing this, the monkey became furious. It shouted angrily at the sparrow, "Fool with a needle face! Are you preaching to me? I don't know how to build a nest. But I know how to tear one up." Then it began to break the sparrows' nests.'

The way Rasathi said those last lines, changing her voice to imitate that of a crow, made me laugh. I asked her to continue.

'After that...like the sparrows here, those sparrows also flew away. Poor things, no, Aunty?'

'Poor things, yes! What can one do? Why did those sparrows have to go and advise that monkey? They should have just made their nests and kept mum.'

'No, Aunty. They gave advice to the monkey only out of sympathy for him, so that he would not get wet in the rain. Tell me, Aunty, how could the monkey do this to them after that?'

'He should not have, but what can we do about it? They say that good things must be told only to good people. Otherwise, this is what happens. One has to be worldly-wise to live in this world or you've had it. No, Rasathi?'

'What are you saying, Aunty? I could not understand

a thing...If we repair this nest, the sparrows may come back, no, Aunty?'

'You may not understand it now, but after you grow up...What did you say? Repair the nest? Seri. Let's do it. You go and bring some straw. We'll arrange it above the damaged nest. The sparrows may come back because of the eggs. In this rain, water may enter the nest, but it won't seep in if we put straw over it.'

Rasathi brought some straw and I arranged it above the nest. Paattiamma, who was watching all this, said, 'The sparrows will never come back if we humans so much as touch their nest. Now those sparrows will build a fresh nest and lay eggs in it. But not here. They'll do it somewhere else.'

'Why won't they come? They will. You just keep an eye out for the crow. The sparrow eggs are in here, so they have to come back.'

I waited every day for the sparrows to return. The rain poured down every day. Rasathi asked me frequently whether the sparrows had come back or not. Days had passed and I had not seen the sparrows. I waited, thinking they might come today or tomorrow. The worrying thought also arose in me that they might never return.

The sparrows never did come back. The rain came down without a break, day and night. I felt sad as I thought how those sparrows must be struggling in all this rain. Rasathi kept nagging me about them. When I told her that the sparrows would never be back, she also felt sad. She asked me, 'Aunty, you have built such a big house. If the sparrows had built their nest inside your house, they would have remained safe inside, no? Even I could have come frequently and watched them. Now the poor things must be getting wet somewhere in the rain. No, Aunty?'

I thought to myself, if they made a nest inside the house, would the old woman let them live in peace?

'Even our house, Aunty, it leaks terribly when it rains. There isn't any dry space on the floor to lie down. My mother places vessels under the roof wherever it leaks. There is only one corner that does not leak. My elder sister Amutha and I curl up there. But my poor mother and father, Aunty, they spend the night without sleep. I wish we had a house like yours that never leaked. I could sleep comfortably with my legs stretched out. No, Aunty?'

What she said churned my heart.

I show so much sympathy for the sparrows, but did I ever bother about these people who live next door? How many times had her mother, Valli, complained to me that their house was leaking terribly...

No. One can't survive in this world with such thoughts in one's mind. I managed to force them out with much effort.

'What's this, Aunty, you have made a hut on your verandah. A small hut like our own house! What's this for, Aunty?' Rasathi asked in surprise.

'This? It's for Baby Jesus. He's going to take birth in this hut tomorrow.'

'Mmmm...Now I understand. You are Christians, Aunty! The kids in my school were talking about it. Lord Jesus is born in such a small hut? When will that be, Aunty? Will you see him?'

'Yes, I'll see him. He's born at midnight.'

'Aunty, me and Amutha—can we sleep over at your house? You have such a big house. Even my mother was asking the other day. She said, "You two go and sleep at Aunty's place when it rains." Shall we come over, Aunty?'

She was almost begging. I kept silent. Many conflicting thoughts passed through my mind: This verandah is vacant. I could let them sleep here. But if I allow them one day, they will keep coming here whenever it rains. It will become a habit. Chi chi...why should I invite such problems for myself? Till now, they slept in their own house. They managed. Why this new desire to come and sleep here now? It was wrong of me to have talked so much with this kid.

When I did not reply, Rasathi asked, 'How much does it cost to build a house that doesn't leak, Aunty? One crore? One lakh?'

'Not so much,' I said abruptly to end the conversation. I felt it would be better if she went away quickly. But it did not look as if she was leaving.

'I will study and get a job and build a house like this. Then you can visit my house, Aunty.'

I just nodded my head.

'Seri, tonight, me and my elder sister will come here to sleep. Tell me what time we should come, Aunty. Immediately after dinner?'

I did not know how to answer her. It seemed like heavy rain was approaching. I asked her to leave and then locked the gate.

ALSO FROM SPEAKING TIGER

THE ADIVASI WILL NOT DANCE
Stories
Hansda Sowvendra Shekhar

'*Shekhar is the sort of writer who appears only rarely in the literary establishment. His voice is powerful, political, urgent. Yet...his concerns are deeply literary, his style, effortless.*' —Scroll.in

In these stories set in the hinterland and small towns of Jharkhand, Hansda Sowvendra Shekhar breathes life into characters who are as robustly flesh and blood as the soil from which they spring, and into which they must sometimes bleed. Troupe-master Mangal Murmu refuses to perform for the President of India and is beaten down; Suren and Gita, a love-blind couple, wait with quiet desperation outside a neonatal ward hoping—for different reasons—that their blue baby will turn pink; Panmuni and Biram Soren move to Vadodara in the autumn of their lives, only to find that they must stop eating meat to be accepted as equal citizens; Talamai Kisku of the Santhal Pargana, migrating to West Bengal in search of work, must sleep with a policeman for fifty rupees and two cold bread pakoras...

The Adivasi Will Not Dance is a mature, passionate, intensely political book, made up of the very stuff of life. It establishes Shekhar as one of India's most important contemporary writers.

'*[Stories] written from the margin, against the grain, and told with great skill and humanity. Hansda Sowvendra Shekhar is a writer to be sought out and discovered.*' —The Indian Express

'*Shekhar's writing brings [us] aspects of India that the grand narratives in Indian English writing have often ignored. Through characters that are powerless in so many ways, and by fusing an indigenous realism to the content of his writing, Shekhar has created a fresh and much-needed idiom for the Indian experience.*' —Deccan Herald

ALSO FROM SPEAKING TIGER

WHEN I HID MY CASTE
Stories
Baburao Bagul

Translated from Marathi by Jerry Pinto

'Originally published in 1963, [Jevha Mi Jaat Chorli Hoti] gifted the nascent Dalit writing tradition with a model of unforgiving honesty of portrayal. In translating the stories, Jerry Pinto retains the earthiness and immediacy of the originals.'—The Telegraph

Baburao Bagul's debut collection of stories revolutionized Marathi Dalit literature, bringing to it raw energy and a radical realism—a refusal to understate or dress up gritty, brutal reality. Through the lives of people on the margins, Bagul exposed the pain, horror and rage of the Dalit experience. The unnamed young protagonist of the title story risks his life and job and conceals his caste from his fellow workers in the hope of bringing about social change. Damu, the village Mahar, demands the right to perform a religious masque—a preserve of the upper castes—thus disrupting the village order. Jaichand Rathod revolts against his parents' wishes and refuses to take up the caste-enforced task of manual scavenging. After years of estrangement, Banoo, a 'kept woman', reaches out to her son who despises her for what she is...

Utterly unsparing in its depiction of the vicious and inhuman caste system, this landmark book is finally available in English, in a brilliant translation by the award-winning author and translator Jerry Pinto.

'[Baburao Bagul] knocked readers off their feet by the sheer elemental force of his stories. But, more importantly, he liberated younger Dalit writers from the shackles of literary Marathi. They say translation gives a classic an afterlife. Jerry Pinto's fluent, empathetic translation has done that for this classic.'—Shanta Gokhale

ALSO FROM SPEAKING TIGER

THE LOST HEROINE
Vinu Abraham
Translated from Malayalam by C.S. Venkiteswaran and Arathy Ashok

Growing up in rural Kerala, Rosy, a poor Dalit Christian girl, had never been to the cinema. Her only brush with fame had been to act in the local Kakkarissi plays. So when Johnson Sir, her well-to-do neighbour, asked if she would like to play the heroine in a movie his friend Daniel was making, Rosy could scarcely believe it. In a matter of weeks, Rosy was transformed into Sarojini—the beautiful Nair girl who lives in a grand tharavad, wears mundus and blouses of the finest silk and gold jewellery from head to toe, and with whom the handsome Jayachandran falls in love at first sight.

But Rosy's dreamworld comes to an end when the last scene of the movie is shot. When the film is screened at the Capitol Theatre in Trivandrum, there is shock and horror in the audience. All hell breaks loose, and Rosy narrowly escapes death, only to spend the rest of her years in anonymity.

Based on the life of the heroine of the first Malayalam film—*Vighathakumaran* (The Lost Child), released in 1928—Vinu Abraham's novel brings alive the world of early Malayalam cinema and the people who pioneered it, weaving within it a poignant story of ambition, desire and the fault lines of caste and religious bigotry.

www.ingramcontent.com/pod-product-compliance
Lightning Source LLC
Chambersburg PA
CBHW011719220426
43663CB00017B/2908